DATE DUE

DEC 2 3 2008

Return Material Promptly

Creation of the Modern Middle East

Palestinian Authority

Creation of the Modern Middle East

Palestinian Authority

John G. Hall

Introduction by
Akbar Ahmed
School of International Service
American University

CHELSEA HOUSE
P U B L I S H E R S
A Haights Cross Communications Company
Philadelphia

Frontispiece: Jericho refugee camp, c. 1992

Cover: For over half a century the conflict between Palestinian Arabs and Palestinian Jews has captured worldwide media attention. To understand the often complex forces behind this ongoing crisis, we must look at the history of the region and its people.

CHELSEA HOUSE PUBLISHERS

VP, NEW PRODUCT DEVELOPMENT Sally Cheney
DIRECTOR OF PRODUCTION Kim Shinners
CREATIVE MANAGER Takeshi Takahashi
MANUFACTURING MANAGER Diann Grasse

Staff for PALESTINIAN AUTHORITY

EDITOR Lee Marcott
PRODUCTION EDITOR Jaimie Winkler
PICTURE RESEARCHER Pat Holl
SERIES AND COVER DESIGNER Keith Trego
LAYOUT 21st Century Publishing and Communications, Inc.

A Haights Cross Communications ◀ Company

http://www.chelseahouse.com

First Printing   3 9082 08828 0477

1 3 5 7 9 8 6 4 2

Library of Congress Cataloging-in-Publication Data
Hall, John G., 1950–
    The Palestinian Authority / John G. Hall.
        v. cm.
Includes bibliographical references and index.
Contents: A short history of Palestine and the Palestinians—Before al-nakbah:
Palestine in the nineteenth century—The conflict takes shape—Palestine and
the British mandate—Palestinian resistance to Israeli occupation—Palestinian
resistance to dispossession—The Arab revolt—The beginning of the end—
The Palestinian Diaspora—Palestine Authority chronology.
    ISBN 0-7910-6515-4
  1. Palestine—History—19th century. 2. Palestine—History—20th century.
3. Jews—Palestine—History—19th century. 4. Jews—Palestine—History—
20th century. 5. Palestinian National Authority. 6. Arab-Israeli conflict.
[1. Palestine—History. 2. Palestinian National Authority. 3. Arab-Israeli
conflict.] I. Title.
DS125 .H28 2002
956.94—dc21
                                                    2002009633

Table of Contents

Index to the Photographs

Creation of the Modern Middle East

Iran

Iraq

Israel

Jordan

The Kurds

Kuwait

Oman

Palestinian Authority

Saudi Arabia

Syria

Turkey

Yemen

Introduction

Akbar Ahmed

The Middle East, it seems, is always in the news. Unfortunately, most of the news is of a troubling kind. Stories of suicide bombers, hijackers, street demonstrations, and ongoing violent conflict dominate these reports. The conflict draws in people living in lands far from the Middle East; some support one group, some support another, often on the basis of kinship or affinity and not on the merits of the case.

The Middle East is often identified with the Arabs. The region is seen as peopled by Arabs speaking Arabic and belonging to the Islamic faith. The stereotype of the Arab oil sheikh is a part of contemporary culture. But both of these images—that the Middle East is in perpetual anarchy and that it has an exclusive Arab identity—are oversimplifications of the region's complex contemporary reality.

In reality, the Middle East is an area that straddles Africa and Asia and has a combined population of over 200 million people inhabiting over twenty countries. It is a region that draws the entire world into its politics and, above all, it is the land that is the birth place of the three great Abrahamic faiths—Judaism, Christianity, and Islam. The city of Jerusalem is the point at which these three faiths come together and also where they tragically confront one another.

It is for these reasons that knowledge of the Middle East will remain of importance and that news from it will remain ongoing and interesting.

Let us consider the stereotype of the Middle East as a land of constant anarchy. It is easy to forget that some of the greatest lawgivers and people of peace were born, lived, and died here. In the Abrahamic tradition these names are a glorious roll call of human history—Abraham, Moses, Jesus, and Muhammad. In the tradition of the Middle East, where these names are especially revered, people often add the blessing "Peace be upon him" when speaking their names.

The land is clearly one that is shared by the great faiths. While it has a dominant Muslim character because of the large Muslim population, its Jewish and Christian presence must not be underestimated. Indeed, it is the dynamics of the relationships between the three faiths that allow us to enter the Middle East today and appreciate the points where these faiths come together or are in conflict.

To understand the predicament in which the people of the Middle East find themselves today, it is well to keep the facts of history before us. History is never far from the minds of the people in this region. Memories of the first great Arab dynasty, the Umayyads (661-750), based in Damascus, and the even greater one of the Abbasids (750-1258), based in Baghdad, are still kept alive in books and folklore. For the Arabs, their history, their culture, their tradition, their language, and above all their religion, provide them with a rich source of pride; but the glory of the past contrasts with the reality and powerlessness of contemporary life.

Many Arabs have blamed past rulers for their current situation beginning with the Ottomans who ruled them until World War I and then the European powers that divided their lands. When they achieved independence after World War II they discovered that the artificial boundaries created by the European powers cut across tribes and clans. Today, too, they complain that a form of Western imperialism still dominates their politics and rulers.

Again, while it is true that Arab history and Arab temperament have colored the Middle East strongly, there are other distinct peoples who have made a significant contribution to the culture of the region. Turkey is one such non-Arab nation with its own language, culture, and contribution to the region through the influence of the Ottoman Empire. Memories of that period for the Arabs are mixed, but what cannot be denied are the spectacular administrative and architectural achievements of the Ottomans. It is the longest dynasty in world history, beginning in 1300 and ending after World War I in 1922, when Kemal Ataturk wished to reject the past on the way to creating a modern Turkey.

Similarly, Iran is another non-Arab country with its own rich language and culture. Based in the minority sect of Islam, the Shia, Iran has often been in opposition to its Sunni neighbors, both Arab and Turk. Perhaps this confrontation helped to forge a unique Iranian, or Persian, cultural identity that, in turn, created the brilliant art, architecture, and poetry under the Safawids (1501-1722). The Safawid period also saw the establishment of the principle of interference or participation—depending on one's perspective—in matters of the state by the religious clerics. So while the Ayatollah Khomeini was very much a late 20th century figure, he was nonetheless reflecting the patterns of Iranian history.

Israel, too, represents an ancient, non-Arabic, cultural and religious tradition. Indeed, its very name is linked to the tribes that figure prominently in the stories of the Bible and it is through Jewish tradition that memory of the great biblical patriarchs like Abraham and Moses is kept alive. History is not a matter of years, but of millennia, in the Middle East.

Perhaps nothing has evoked as much emotional and political controversy among the Arabs as the creation of the state of Israel in 1948. With it came ideas of democracy and modern culture that seemed alien to many Arabs. Many saw the wars that followed stir further conflict and hatred; they also saw the wars as an inevitable clash between Islam and Judaism.

It is therefore important to make a comment on Islam and Judaism. The roots of prejudice against Jews can be anti-Semitic, anti-Judaic, and anti-Zionist. The prejudice may combine all three and there is often a degree of overlap. But in the case of the Arabs, the matter is more complicated because, by definition, Arabs cannot be anti-Semitic because they themselves are considered Semites. They cannot be anti-Judaic, because Islam recognizes the Jews as "people of the Book."

What this leaves us with is the clash between the political philosophy of Zionism, which is the establishment of a Jewish nation in Palestine, and Arab thought. The antagonism of the Arabs to Israel may result in the blurring of lines. A way must be found by Arabs and Israelis to live side by side in peace. Perhaps recognition of the common Abrahamic tradition is one way forward.

The hostility to Israel partly explains the negative coverage the Arabs get in the Western media. Arab Muslims are often accused of being anarchic and barbaric due to the violence of the Middle East. Yet, their history has produced some of the greatest figures in history.

Consider the example of Sultan Salahuddin Ayyoubi, popularly called Saladin in Western literature. Saladin had vowed to take revenge for the bloody massacres that the Crusaders had indulged in when they took Jerusalem in 1099. According to a European eyewitness account the blood in the streets was so deep that it came up to the knees of the horsemen.

Yet, when Saladin took Jerusalem in 1187, he showed the essential compassion and tolerance that is at the heart of the Abrahamic faiths. He not only released the prisoners after ransom, as was the custom, but paid for those who were too poor to afford any ransom. His nobles and commanders were furious that he had not taken a bloody revenge. Saladin is still remembered in the bazaars and villages as a leader of great learning and compassion. When contemporary leaders are compared to Saladin, they are usually found wanting. One reason may be that the problems of the region are daunting.

The Middle East faces three major problems that will need solutions in the twenty-first century. These problems affect society and politics and need to be tackled by the rulers in those lands and all other people interested in creating a degree of dialogue and participation.

The first of the problems is that of democracy. Although democracy is practiced in some form in a number of the Arab countries, for the majority of ordinary people there is little sense of participation in their government. The frustration of helplessness in the face of an indifferent bureaucracy at the lower levels of administration is easily converted to violence. The indifference of the state to the pressing needs of the "street" means that other non-governmental organizations can step in. Islamic organizations offering health and education programs to people in the shantytowns and villages have therefore emerged and flourished over the last decades.

The lack of democracy also means that the ruler becomes remote and autocratic over time as he consolidates his power. It is not uncommon for many rulers in the Middle East to pass on their rule to their son. Dynastic rule, whether kingly or based in a dictatorship, excludes ordinary people from a sense of participation in their own governance. They need to feel empowered. Muslims need to feel that they are able to participate in the process of government. They must feel that they are able to elect their leaders into office and if these leaders do not deliver on their promises, that they can throw them out. Too many of the rulers are nasty and brutish. Too many Muslim leaders are kings and military dictators. Many of them ensure that their sons or relatives stay on to perpetuate their dynastic rule.

With democracy, Muslim peoples will be able to better bridge the gaps that are widening between the rich and the poor. The sight of palatial mansions with security guards carrying automatic weapons standing outside them and, alongside, hovels teeming with starkly poor children is a common one in Muslim cities. The distribution of wealth must remain a priority of any democratic government.

The second problem in the Middle East that has wide ramifications in society is that of education. Although Islam emphasizes knowledge and learning, the sad reality is that the standards of education are unsatisfactory. In addition, the climate for scholarship and intellectual activity is discouraging. Scholars are too often silenced, jailed, or chased out of the country by the administration. The sycophants and the intelligence services whose only aim is to tell the ruler what he would like to hear, fill the vacuum.

Education needs to be vigorously reformed. The *madrassah,* or religious school, which is the institution that provides primary education for millions of boys in the Middle East, needs to be brought into line with the more prestigious Westernized schools reserved for the elite of the land. By allowing two distinct streams of education to develop, Muslim nations are encouraging the growth of two separate societies: a largely illiterate and frustrated population that is susceptible to leaders with simple answers to the world's problems and a small, Westernized, often corrupt and usually uncaring group of elite. The third problem facing the Middle East is that of representation in the mass media. Although this point is hard to pin down, the images in the media are creating problems of understanding and communication in the communities living in the Middle East. Muslims, for example, will always complain that they are depicted in negative stereotypes in the non-Arab media. The result of the media onslaught that plagues Muslims is the sense of anger on the one hand and the feeling of loss of dignity on the other. Few Muslims will discuss the media rationally. Greater Muslim participation in the media and greater interaction will help to solve the problem. But it is not so simple. The Israelis also complain of the stereotypes in the Arab media that depict them negatively.

Muslims are aware that their religious culture represents a civilization rich in compassion and tolerance. They are aware that given a period of stability in which they can grapple with the problems of democracy, education, and self-image they can take their rightful place in the community of nations. However painful the current reality, they do carry an idea of an ideal human society with them. Whether a Turk, or an Iranian, or an Arab, every Muslim is aware of the message that the prophet of Islam brought to this region in the seventh century. This message still has resonance for these societies. Here are words from the last address of the prophet spoken to his people:

> All of you descend from Adam and Adam was made of earth. There is no superiority for an Arab over a non-Arab nor for a non-Arab over an Arab, neither for a white man over a black man nor a black man over a white man . . . the noblest among you is the one who is most deeply conscious of God.

This is a noble and worthy message for the twenty-first century in the Middle East. Not only Muslims, but Jews, and Christians would agree with it. Perhaps its essential theme of tolerance, compassion, and equality can help to rediscover the wellsprings of tradition that can both inspire and unite.

It is for these reasons that I congratulate Chelsea House Publishers for taking the initiative in helping us to understand the Middle East through this series. The story of the Middle East is, in many profound ways, the story of human civilization.

— **Dr. Akbar S. Ahmed**
  The Ibn Khaldun Chair of Islamic Studies and
  Professor of International Relations,
  School of International Service
  American University

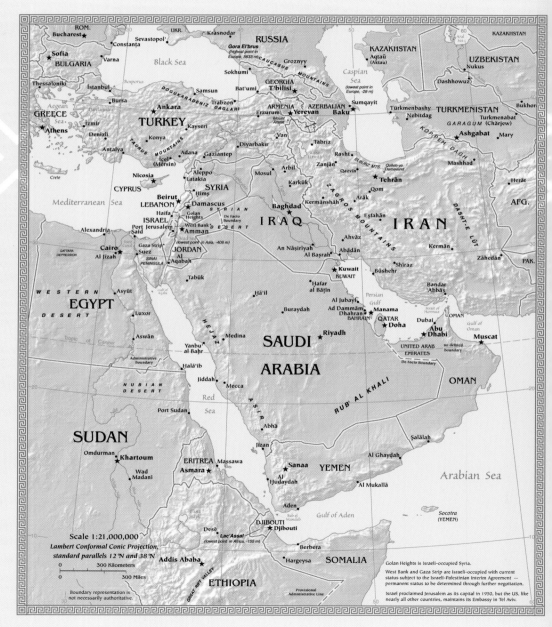

Modern Map of the Middle East

ISRAEL & NEIGHBORS

LEBANON

SYRIA

Beirut⊗

U.N. Zones

Mediterranean

⊗ Damascus

Sea

Golan
Heights

Israeli-held
Zone

Tel Aviv-
Jaffa●

West
Bank

⊗ Amman

Jerusalem⊗

Gaza
Strip

Dead
Sea

ISRAEL

JORDAN

N

EGYPT

Sinai
Peninsula

| 0 | | | 75 km |
| 0 | | | 75 mi |

SAUDI
ARABIA

©1995 MAGELLAN Geographix℠ Santa Barbara, CA 1-800-929-4627

Modern Map of Israel and its Bordering Countries

The Negev Desert

The Southern Desert or Negev region comprises nearly half the land of Palestine.

1

A Short History of Palestine and the Palestinians

o you or your family subscribe to a local newspaper? Do you watch the morning or evening news on your local channels, or perhaps you prefer the short clips served up as "news briefs" on MTV. Have you ever read or just leafed through *Time*, *Newsweek*, or *People* magazine, while sitting in the waiting room at the dentist's office or standing in line at the local supermarket. If so, then you have been bombarded with images and headlines of the "Crisis in the Middle East," particularly the conflict between the Palestinians and the Israelis. Pick up almost any newspaper or magazine, turn on any morning or evening news broadcast and you will see a sampling of the following headlines: "Announcement of U.S. peace trip followed by deadly clashes," "Deadly day of conflict,"

Terror attacks kill 14 Israelis," "Israeli tanks surround Arafat." Even during one of America's greatest national catastrophes, September 11, 2001, when every radio, television, newspaper, and magazine reported the tragedy of the World Trade Center and the Pentagon, images from the Middle East filtered through the airways as if the conflicts in the Middle East and our own public and private tragedies were somehow interrelated, as if our two histories suddenly collided and images of an American tragedy and images of the crisis in the Middle East were competing for space in the same headlines. But why? How is it possible for a country the size of Vermont to demand so much of our public and private attention. And that is just what it has done. For the past fifty-four years the conflict between the Palestinian Arabs and the Palestinian Jews have demanded constant media attention, not just in America but throughout the world. However, even though the Middle Eastern crisis has demanded and received constant media attention and even though our imaginations have become saturated with images and headlines it doesn't mean that we are any closer to understanding the "real" stories, the "real" sacrifices, and the tragic loss of human lives that has become part of the permanent landscape.

Many scholars and historians trace the source of this conflict to 1948. That was the year the State of Israel was founded. An occasion that was immediately marked by a war between the Arabs in the Middle East and the new State of Israel. Judging from these circumstances it would seem that the scholars and historians are right, the founding of the State of Israel triggered the conflict between the Arabs and Jews that has lasted for the past fifty-four years. And on some level that observation would be accurate, especially when you consider all the supporting information. But on the other hand, this explanation, regardless of its accuracy, doesn't tell the entire story. Because the images and head-lines that erupt out of the Middle East on an almost daily basis have a much longer history that began in ancient times, over three thousand years ago. As a result, to fully appreciate the nature of the conflict it would be beneficial to explore the history of Palestine and the people who have inhabited the land since ancient times.

The historic region known as Palestine covers a total area of approximately 10,435 square miles. It is about the size of Vermont, one of the smallest states in the United States. The region has an extremely diverse terrain and, generally speaking, may be divided into four parallel zones. From west to east are the coastal planes. These consist of fertile land with an abundance of underground water and abundant rainfall. These plains have always been highly developed and contained large stretches of citrus groves.

The hill region is predominantly rock but is suitable for planting deciduous trees. The olive is its principal crop. In winter, large acres of land are planted with wheat and barley, and in summer, corn, tomatoes, and other vegetables are grown under dry-farming cultivation.

The Jordan Valley region lies below sea level where the soil is suitable for most kinds of cultivation, especially citrus and tropical fruits. However, since there is insufficient rainfall, farmers depend on irrigation from streams or water is pumped from the Jordan River.

Finally, The Southern Desert or Negev region comprises nearly half the land of Palestine. The northern section consists of rich soil and is suitable for irrigation. The southern part consists of deeply eroded uplands and rift valleys.

The word Palestine derives from "Philistia," the name given by Greek writers to the land of the "Philistines," who in the twelfth century B.C. occupied a small stretch of land on the southern coast between modern Tel Aviv, Yafo and Gaza. The name was revived by the Romans in the second century A.D., when they referred to the region as "Syria Palaestina."

Citrus stand in Jericho

Although Palestine is about the size of Vermont, its terrain is quite diverse. Many think of the region as being a desert, but in the coastal plains there is enough rainfall and underground water to sustain rich citrus groves and other crops.

The earliest known inhabitants of Palestine were the Canaanites. During the third millennium B.C. they lived in city-states, the most notable of which was Jericho. They developed an alphabet, and their religion was a major influence on the beliefs and practices of Judaism, Christianity, and Islam.

Palestine's location, at the center of routes linking three continents, made it the meeting place for religious and cultural influences from Egypt, Syria, Mesopotamia, and Asia Minor. It was also the natural battleground for the great powers of the region and subject to domination by adjacent empires, beginning with Egypt in the third millennium B.C.

After the Egyptians had conquered the Canaanites, their control and domination of the region was constantly challenged by an ethnically diverse group of invaders, including the Amorites, Hittites, and the Hurrians. These invaders, however, were defeated by the Egyptians and absorbed by the Canaanites. Gradually, as Egyptian influence declined new invaders appeared. Most notable among these were the Hebrews, a term, which means, "Those who pass from place to place." The Hebrews were a group of Semitic tribes that, according to tradition, migrated from Mesopotamia to Palestine during the second millennium B.C. However, some scholars trace their origin to "the wilderness," the Sinai, rather than Mesopotamia. The other groups of invaders were the Philistines, highly civilized inhabitants of the coastal region of Palestine.

This was also the group after whom the country was later named. They lived on the coast of the Mediterranean Sea, to the southeast of Judea, a part of what is now the West Bank. According to the Old Testament (Amos 9:7, Jeremiah 47:4, and Deuteronomy 2:23) they came from Caphtor, which modern scholars identify with Crete (Kriti).

Hebrew tribes probably immigrated to the region centuries before Moses led his people out of slavery in Egypt in about 1270 B.C. But, according to tradition, the Hebrews, or the Twelve Tribes of Israel, finally defeated the Canaanites about 1125 B.C., but they found the struggle with the Philistines more difficult. The Philistines had established an independent state on the southern coast of Palestine and controlled a number of towns to the north and east. Superior in military organization and using iron weapons, they severely defeated the Hebrews about 1050 B.C. The Philistine threat forced the Hebrews to unite and establish a monarchy, Saul was the first King of ancient Israel, but it was David who finally defeated the Philistines shortly after 1000 B.C.

The unity of Israel and the gradual decline of other empires enabled David to establish a large independent state, with its capital at Jerusalem. After David's death his son Solomon was the next great King of Israel. During his reign the region enjoyed peace and prosperity, but after his death in 922 B.C. the Kingdom was divided into Israel in the north and Judah in the south. The divided Israelites could no longer maintain their independence. Israel fell to Assyria in 722 and 721 B.C., and Judah was conquered by Babylonia in 586 B.C. As a result of this conquest, Jerusalem was destroyed and the Jews were exiled.

When Cyrus the Great of Persia conquered Babylonia in 539 B.C. he permitted the Jews to return to Judea, a district of Palestine. Under Persian rule the Jews were allowed considerable autonomy, they rebuilt the walls of Jerusalem and codified the Mosaic law, the Torah, which became the code of social life and religious observance.

Persian domination of Palestine was replaced by Greek rule when Alexander the Great of Macedonia conquered the region in 333 B.C. Alexander's successors, the Ptolemy's of Egypt and the Seleucids of Syria, ruled the country. The Seleucids tried to impose Hellenistic (Greek) culture and religion on the population. This led to a series of revolts by

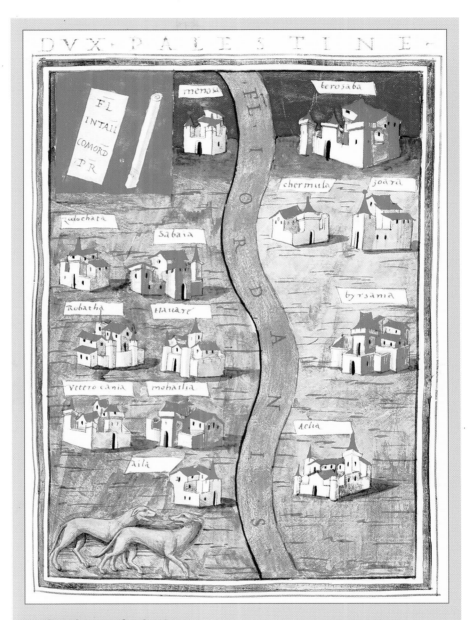

Medieval Map of Palestine

For centuries, Palestine has stood at the center of major trade and travel routes between Europe, Africa, and Asia. Since the third century B.C., it has been a battleground for the great powers of the region seeking to control these routes.

the Jewish inhabitants. The Maccabees revolted and set up an independent state, which lasted approximately eighty years, until Pompey the Great conquered Palestine for Rome and made it a province ruled by Jewish Kings. It was during the rule of King Herod the Great, (37–4 B.C.), that Jesus was born.

Two more Jewish revolts were suppressed in the following years. After the second revolt, numerous Jews were killed and many of the survivors were sold into slavery. It was during this time that Judea was renamed Syria Palaestina.

Palestine received special attention when the Roman Emperor Constantine made Christianity the official religion of the Roman Empire in A.D. 313. His mother, Helena, visited Jerusalem and Palestine and from that time the region was looked upon as the Holy Land and became the focus of Christian pilgrimage. A golden age of prosperity, security, and culture followed. Most of the population became Hellenized and Christianized. Byzantine (Roman) rule was interrupted, however, by a brief Persian occupation of Palestine in 614–629 and was ended altogether when Muslim Arabs invaded Palestine and captured Jerusalem in A.D. 638.

The Arab conquest began 1300 years of Muslim occupation of what then became known as "Filastin." Palestine was holy to Muslims because, according to their tradition, the Prophet Muhammad designated Jerusalem as the first "gibla" the direction Muslims face when praying, and because he was believed to have ascended on the night journey to heaven from the area of Solomon's temple, where the Dome of the Rock was later built. After Mecca and Medina, Jerusalem became the third holiest city of Islam.

The Muslim rulers did not force their religion on the Palestinians, and more than a century passed before the majority converted to Islam. The remaining Christians and

Jews were considered "People of the Book." They were allowed control of their own communities and permitted freedom of worship. The majority of Palestinians also adopted Arabic and Islamic culture.

Many Muslims generally consider the first four caliphs, successors to Muhammad, as the golden age of Islam. Muhammad died in 632 leaving no instructions for the future government of the Muslim community. A group of Islamic leaders met in Medina (now in Saudi Arabia,) the capital of the Muslim world at that time, and elected Abu Bakr, the Prophet's father-in-law and closest associate, to lead the community. Abu Bakr adopted the title "Khalifat Rasul Allah," an Arabic expression meaning "successor to the Messenger of God," from which the term "caliph," Khalifah or "successor" is derived.

Umar I became the second Caliph in 634. On his deathbed, Abu Bakr designated Umar as his successor, and other members of the Muslim Community accepted Umar's succession. Under his leadership, the great expansion of Islam took place. Egypt, Syria, Iraq, and the northern part of Mesopotamia became Islamic territories, and the armies of the Persian Empire were routed several times. Umar added the title amir-al-mum-inin or "commander of the believers," to that of caliph.

After Umar's death in 644, Uthman ibn Affan, Muhammad's son-in-law and one of his first converts, was appointed the third caliph. Although an elderly man, he carried on Umar's policy of territorial expansion. It wasn't long, however, before Uthman alienated many of his subjects, who felt he favored the aristocracy in Mecca in political and commercial affairs. Rebellious Muslim troops from Al Kufah (Iraq) and Egypt besieged Uthman in Medina and assassinated him in 656.

The Medinians and the rebellious troops acknowledged Ali, a cousin and son-in-law of Muhammad, as the fourth caliph. However, the governor of Syria, Mu'awiyah, later Mu'awiyah I the first Umayyad Caliph, refused to recognize Ali as Caliph and called for vengeance for the death of Uthman, who was related to Mu'awiyah. In 657 the rival parties met at Siffin, on a plain in Northern Syria near the site of the modern city Ar Raggah. After an inconclusive battle, they agreed to arbitrate the dispute. Angered by this decision, and with Ali for submitting to it, a group of his followers known as the Kharijites, vowed to assassinate both Ali and Mu'awiyah. They succeeded only in killing Ali, and in 661, after a brief dispute with Hasan, Ali's son, Mu'awiyah was proclaimed the fourth Caliph.

Mu'awiyah was the first in a long line of Umayyad Caliphs, whose reign lasted from 661 to 750. During his reign he stabilized the Muslim community after Ali's death. He moved the capital of Islam from Medina to Damascus, bringing the Muslim rulers into close contact with the cultural and administrative traditions of the Byzantine Empire.

Palestine benefited from the empire's trade and from its religious importance during the Umayyad Dynasty. It shared in the glory of Muslim civilization, especially when the Muslim world enjoyed a golden age in science, art, philosophy, and literature. Muslims preserved Greek learning and broke new ground in several fields, all of which later contributed to the Renaissance in Europe. However, when power shifted to Baghdad with the Abbasid Caliphs in 750, Palestine became neglected. It suffered unrest and successive domination by Seljuks, Fatimids, and European crusaders, and like the rest of the empire, Palestine gradually stagnated and declined under Mamluks rule.

The Ottoman Empire defeated the Mamluks in 1517 and with few interruptions, ruled Palestine until the winter of 1918. The country was divided into several districts or "Sanjaks," such as that of Jerusalem. The administration of the districts was largely left to the responsibility of the

Palestinian Arabs who were descendants of the Canaanites and other successive settlers. The Christian and Jewish communities were granted a large degree of freedom. Palestine shared in the glory of the Ottoman Empire during the sixteenth century, but declined when the empire started to decline in the seventeenth century.

The decline of Palestine, in trade, agriculture, and population continued until the nineteenth century. At that time the search by Europeans powers for raw materials and markets, as well as their strategic interest, brought them to the Middle East.

Al-Aqsa Mosque with Dome of the Rock, c. 1992

As far back as the 19th century, colonial disputes among British, French, Ottoman, Russian, and other forces have shaped the social and economic environment of Palestine—a land where Muslims, Jews, and Christians had long coexisted. The Dome of the Rock is the place where the Prophet Muhammad is believed by Muslims to have ascended into heaven.

2

Before al-Nakbah: Palestine in the 19th Century

The modern history of Palestine begins around 1800 at the beginning of the nineteenth century, and ends in 1948, the year following World War II. For Palestinians, this period is known as the time before "Al-Nakbah," or "the time before the catastrophic destruction of Palestine." These years can be divided into two main historical periods. The first covers the nineteenth century and World War I, and the second begins after World War II, with the establishment of the British Mandate of Palestine under the authority of The League of Nations.

Additional historical events transpired during the one hundred and forty-eight years before Al-Nakbah, that were destined to have a profound impact on Palestine and the Palestinian Arabs who lived there. Foremost among these was the expansion of the British Colonial Empire. During the nineteenth century Britain was the dominant economic and political power in the world. As a result, Britain faced little competition from the other European powers. Left unchallenged, they were able to extend their power through informal influence without necessarily asserting formal political control, which would add to the administrative cost and other responsibilities. This push for informal influence became known as the "imperialism of free trade." The British did not establish many formal colonies, but they controlled other nations in order to exercise their economic power. In the Middle East, for example, the British wished to maintain the political stability of the region and, if possible to continue the sovereignty of the Ottoman Empire in order to ensure the safety of their routes to India across Ottoman lands. They attempted for most of the nineteenth century to remain on friendly terms with the Ottomans in order to block any ambitions of their European rivals and keep open their lines of communication to the east. This British policy was part of what has been called "The Great Game in Asia." In the long run, this policy of "European intervention" transformed the social, economic, political, and cultural structure of Palestine, with devastating consequences for the indigenous Arab population of the country.

The other historical event that had lasting consequences for the Palestinians was the rise of European nationalism, which led to the intensification of anti-Semitism during the latter half of the nineteenth century. This in turn led to increased immigration to Palestine and the birth of the "World Zionist Organization," which was created to solve Europe's "Jewish problem." These factors set in motion many of the antagonisms that have lasted until the present day, and continue to shape attitudes and events in the region, Israel, the occupied territories of the West Bank and Gaza Strip, and among Palestinians in exile.

European intervention in Palestine encouraged the process of European settlement in the country, transformed the economy, created new social classes, and rearranged power relationships among existing social groups, including recent Jewish settlers. For example, as a result of European intervention, Christian and Jews were granted effective political and religious equality with Muslims, thus over-turning the foundations and structure of Muslim society that had been in place for centuries. As already stated to Muslims, Christian and Jews are regarded as "People of the Book," believers in God, revelation and the day- of-judgment. As such, they were not to be persecuted or forced to become Muslims. No attempt was made to subject them to the Muslim legal code; they were left free to regulate their own communal and personal life in accordance with their own religious laws.

At the same time, however, they were not considered to be on equal status with their Muslim counterparts. In fact, they were considered a special category within Muslim society and were referred to as "dhimmis," or non-Muslims. They were also expected to pay specified taxes, the "jizya," a poll tax paid by all non-Muslims, and the "kharaj," a property tax that was paid by everybody, including Muslims.

This customary view of a world in which "dhimmis" remained in inferior positions befitting their status, was turned upside down by European intervention. The improved status of Christians and Jews seemed to many Muslims to be instigated by hostile forces that sought to weaken Muslim control over lands they considered to be their own. Muslim resentment toward Christians was further intensified because European consuls and traders hired Christians to represent them in the selling of European goods that were cheaper than the products sold by Muslim merchants.

The local market on which Muslims relied was thus undermined to the benefit of Europeans and their Christian protégés, who usually acquired protective status "barat," and became exempt from Muslim authority. What made matters worse was the manner in which some Christian clergy flaunted their newfound equality by holding public processions in elaborate vestments and having church bells rung, practices forbidden under Muslim ordinances for centuries.

The process of intervention began slowly during the first decades of the nineteenth century but increased by mid-century, especially after the Crimean War (1853–1856). The war arose from the conflict of the "great powers," (Russian, French, British, Ottoman,) in the Middle East and was more directly caused by Russian demands to exercise protection over the Orthodox Christians under Ottoman authority. Another major factor was the dispute between Russia and France over privileges of the Russian Orthodox and Roman Catholic Churches in the holy places in Palestine.

The Crimean War was managed and commanded poorly on both sides. Disease accounted for a disproportionate number of the approximately 250,000 men lost by each side. Its' conclusion was marked by the signing of The Treaty of Paris on March 30, 1856, which proved a major setback for Russia's Middle Eastern policy. The Ottoman Empire, in taking part in the treaty signing promised to respect the rights of all its Christian subjects. Although, on the surface it appeared a minor concession, it nevertheless served to heighten the prestige and self-esteem of the Christians living in the Middle East, especially in relation to their Arab neighbors. In a very real sense this set the stage for the great deluge, which was less than thirty years away.

As previously stated, although the consequences of European intervention were initially small and incremental, they later became large and wrenching. Over the century and a half, from the beginning of the nineteenth century to

Turkish soldiers in the Crimean War, c. 1855

The Crimean War (1853-1856) resulted from an attempt by Russia to protect Orthodox Christians living under Ottoman (Turkish) authority, and marked the first in a series of outside interventions that would end the existence of Palestine as an independent nation. This drawing from 1855 shows a Turkish contingent for the war.

the final destruction of Palestine, the Palestinian people witnessed many great industrial, technological, political, economic, social, and cultural changes. However, very few, if any of them, were meant for their advantage. Economic activity and productivity in trade, agriculture, industry, and services increased substantially but became more and more dependent on Europe, especially Great Britain, the dominant colonial power. In other words, European intervention propelled the people of Palestine from a largely subsistence and semi-feudal existence into a market economy completely dependent on European trade and capital investment.

Throughout this "wrenching" transformation Palestinian peasants clung to their land, their villages, their families, and their identity. But their attempts to preserve their traditional way of life, the only way of life they had known from time immemorial, proved to be nothing more than futile gestures. Because once the "invisible hand," European intervention had set in motion, the tide sweeping Palestine towards its inevitable destruction could not be stayed. It was as relentless and inexorable as the passage of time. And it seemed that no power on earth was great enough to halt or reverse the trend. Based on this observation, it can be argued that European intervention created the conditions for the gradual and inevitable destruction of Palestine and the dispossession of its people long before the actual event took place in 1948, the year of al-Nakbah.

Equally significant, was the so-called peaceful crusade of religiously inspired European immigration, investment, and institutional development. More specifically, French Catholics participated in what they called "the peaceful crusade," visiting holy places and donating substantial sums to build religious institutions. The German Templars established agricultural colonies with the idea of settling in Palestine and Christianizing it if possible. Finally, Protestant missionaries from Europe and America came to Palestine. They sought converts among members of other Christian sects and encouraged Jewish immigration. As evangelical Christians who considered the end of the world to be close at hand, they hoped to bring Jews to Palestine and convert them to Christianity in the Holy Land prior to the "Day of Judgment."

Just as important was the increase in modern education, which was accompanied by drastic changes in social values,

Palestinian Children Doing Lessons Outside

Among Europe's influences on Palestine was the introduction of more modern educational methods. With the underlying aim of creating new converts to Christianity, however, missionaries unwittingly triggered a fierce wave of Islamic nationalism.

norms, and life styles. Following these changes, and perhaps even inspired by them, was the birth of Arab and Palestinian nationalism and Islamic consciousness. Historically, the tendency toward nationalism was fostered by the various technological, cultural, political, and economic advances. Improvements in communications extended the knowledge of people, their village and province, and the spread of education gave them a feeling of participation in a common cultural heritage. Through education, people learned of their common background and tradition and began to identify themselves with the historical continuity of the group or nation, which gave them a sense of helping to determine their fate as a nation and of sharing responsibility for the future well being of that nation. And all of this occurred in the context of a rapidly increasing population, both from natural increase and, to a lesser extent, because of immigration of European Christians and Jews, which drastically altered the composition of the country.

Looked at in this context, Arab and Palestinian nationalism is a product of and a reaction to European intervention, for after all it was European intervention that transformed the economy, created new social classes, and rearranged power relationships among groups. It had also been European interventionism that introduced the majority of technological, cultural, and political advances. And, even though these changes would, in the long run, hasten the demise of traditional Palestinian society, it would in the meantime provide them with the necessary tools to build a defense against the onslaught of changes that suddenly and irrevocable assailed their lives. In the nineteenth century their most important defense was their growing sense of nationalism.

This growing sense of nationalism or self-awareness should not be underestimated, especially in regards to the indigenous people of Palestine. In their history, culture, and religion, Palestine and the Palestinians have long been an integral part of the Arab and Islamic world. For centuries, the country and its people have been the geographical and social bridge connecting the "Mahreq" or "The Arab East" to Egypt and the "Maghreb" or "The Arab West." Palestinians are related by kinship, economic, religious, and political ties to the people of Lebanon and Syria to the north, Jordan, and Iraq to the east, Saudi Arabia to the southeast, and Egypt to the west.

Granted, of course, this growing sense of self-awareness was still in its infancy during the early part of the nineteenth century, but over time, especially the latter half of the century and the first decades of the twentieth century it steadily picked up momentum. And it continued to spread and take root until, by the time of the destruction of Palestine and the dispersal of its people, it had become of central importance, influencing the political and economic dynamics of the eastern Arab world. In fact, this penetrating sense of self-awareness along with the so-called Palestinian Question (some might say "problem") has become a formative issue or determining factor not only in regard to conflicts between states in the region but also between contending political groups and between regimes and the people within many states. Likewise, furthermore, the "Palestinian Question" or "the cause of Palestine" has become central to both secular, (nationalist and radicals) and religious political and ideological movements.

As stated earlier, this awakened national sensibility on the part of Arabs and Palestinians was accompanied by a corresponding rise in Islamic consciousness. In fact, one of the most powerful ideological concerns regarding Palestine involved religion. Islam views Palestine as sacred. The Qur'an (Koran) refers to the country as "al-Ardal-Mugaddasah," meaning "the Holy Land." Al-Khalil (Hebron) and al-Quds (Jerusalem) are sacred cities. The Ibrahimi Mosque in al-Khalil is the site of the grave of the prophet Abraham (Ibrahim, in Arabic). Al-Quds is the site of al-Haram al-Sharif (the Noble Sanctuary) upon Temple Mount, the third holiest shrine of Islam, after Mecca and Medina. The Noble Sanctuary includes al-Masjed al-Aqsa and the Qubbat al-Sakhra (Dome of the Rock) mosques. It is from the Dome of the Rock during the night of al-Mi'raj that the prophet Muhammad miraculously ascended to heaven upon the winged stallion al-Buraq. Al-Quds and al-Ard al-Muqaddash of Filastin (Palestine) are powerful symbols of identity for Muslim individuals and the entire Islamic "umma" or nation or community of believers.

Following the Crimean War, Palestine became even more susceptible to European interventionism. From approximately mid-century to the beginning of World War I, European colonists settled in Palestine, which accelerated the integration of the country into European economy. Initially, however, small numbers of Muslim immigrants entered the country from formerly held Ottoman Territories. There were North Africans fleeing French colonization in Algiers and Morocco, Bosnians fleeing Austrian repression in Yugoslavia, and Circassian refugees from the Russian Caucasus. As stated earlier, they arrived in relatively small numbers but more importantly, for the stability of the region, they assimilated quickly into the culture and society of Palestine.

Unlike their Muslim counterparts, Christian and Jewish immigrants had a different religious and ideological motivation for coming to Palestine. They came, not as refugees seeking sanctuary, but as Crusaders, Salvationists, and Redeemers. They came to rescue the Holy Land. For example, the "Tempelgesellschaft" "Association of Templars," a Protestant Piestic religious movement from the German Kingdom of Wurttemberg, came to "rescue humankind from the anti-Christian spirit." Their leaders preached the creation of "the people of God," and they assembled in Jerusalem to regain control of Paletine as heirs to the Promised Land.

Perhaps more important for Palestine and the Palestinians was the rapid increase of Jewish immigrants. This came after the establishment of the World Zionist Organization.

Prior to that time, Jewish settlement was spontaneous and intermittent. But, following the *pogroms*, or persecution of Jews, in Eastern Europe and Russia, and the formal launching of the Zionist movement settlement activity became more systematic and expansive. The Zionist movement was an organized movement of world Jewry that arose in Europe in the nineteenth century with the aim of reclaiming Palestine as a Jewish state. So began a process that would culminate in violent conflicts late in the nineteenth century and continuing throughout the twentieth century.

Mountains Reflected in the Dead Sea

The beauty of the Palestinian landscape belies the region's troubled history. As Muslims, Christians, and Jews crowded together in the region, tensions between these religious ideologies began to increase.

3
The Conflict Takes Shape

"Zionism" is a Jewish Nationalist movement created to unite the Jewish people of the *"Diaspora"* (exile) and settle them in Palestine, the ancient homeland of the Jews, which is called *"Eretz Israel"* in Hebrew. The movement was born in the latter half of the nineteenth century and culminated in 1948 with the creation of the State of Israel. The movement's name is derived from the word Zion, the ancient Hebrew name for the easternmost hill of the city of Jerusalem, known today as the Temple Mount. In 1000 B.C. King David captured Zion and made it the center of the political and cultural life of the ancient Hebrew. Eventually Zion became a designation for all Jerusalem and Palestine. After the fall of Judea in A.D. 70, Zion became the

43

symbol of the hope that the Jewish homeland in Palestine eventually would be restored. Over the centuries the Jews of the Diaspora associated the hope of the return with the coming of the *"Messiah,"* a savior whom God would send to deliver them. As we have already seen, prior to the nineteenth century, small numbers of Jews often migrated to Palestine to join Jewish communities that continued to exist there, but they remained a small minority among a largely Palestinian Arab population.

However, in the latter half of the nineteenth century this all changed. It was during this period that the modern Zionist movement was born. It was inspired primarily by the rise of nationalism and anti-Semitism in Eastern and Western Europe. In the second half of the century organized anti-Semitic parties emerged in Germany and Austria-Hungary. Also, in Russia, the assassination of Tsar Alexander II in 1881, unleashed a wave of nationalist feeling, and anti-Jewish riots or pogroms. The Tsar was killed with a bomb thrown by a member of the *Narodnaya Volya,* or *"Land and Freedom"* movement, a nineteenth-century Russian revolutionary organization that regarded terrorist activities as the best means of forcing political reform. Although, the assassin was not Jewish, rumors spread that Jews were responsible for the death of Alexander. As a result, mobs in more than two hundred cities and towns attacked Jewish people and destroyed their homes and property. The result was that by the beginning of World War I, a vast migration movement of over a million and a half Jews left Russia. The great majority headed for the United States but others set their sights and hopes on Palestine.

This movement, this first wave of immigration, took the name of *"BILU,"* derived from a passage in Isaiah that reads, "Bet Ya'acov lechu ve nelcha" or "O House of Jacob, come ye, and let us go." The efforts of Zionism to colonize Palestine are usually dated from the arrival of the *"Biluim,"* they initiated the first of five identifiable waves of Jewish immigration to Palestine in modern times.

Some Russian Jews also began to think about migration to Palestine during this period and turned to the ideas being advanced by intellectuals such as Moshe Leib Lilienblum and Leo Pinsker, who were the major contributors to Zionist thought and ideology during this initial phase. In his, *Let Us Not Confuse the Issues,* Lilienblum wrote "Let us gather our dispersed from Eastern Europe and go up to our kind with rejoicing, whoever is on the side of God and his people, let him say, 'I am for Zion'."

Leo Pinsker stated similar themes in his widely read pamphlet *Auto-Emancipation: An Appeal to His People by a Russian Jew.* Although Palestine was less central in his thinking, Pinsker embraced the idea of Jewish nationalism and pleaded for a Jewish national home.

The writings of these two men and others became the philosophical foundation for such organizations as the *Hovevei Zion,* or the *"Lovers of Zion."* Lilienblum even became a leader of the Hovevei Zion movement, which collected money, offered courses in Hebrew and Jewish history, and provided instruction in self-defense, all of which was viewed as preparation for immigration to Palestine.

Although less violent than Tsarist Russia, anti-Semitism was also on the rise in Western Europe. In Germany, for example, economic disorder following the Franco-Prussian War, and the economic crisis of 1873 led to charges that the country was being undermined by corrupt Jewish financiers. In response to the involvement of some Jews in the many scandals that were uncovered, an onslaught of anti-Semitic literature began to appear. In fact, the term "anti-Semitism" was coined in 1879 by the German agitator Wilhelm Marr to designate the anti-Jewish campaigns then underway in Central Europe.

Anti-Semitism was also on the rise in France, which set

in motion several events that would have a direct impact on the Zionist movement. One of these critical events was the trial and conviction of Captain Alfred Dreyfus, a Jewish officer who had risen to a position of importance in the French army. In 1894, he was accused of spying for Germany, and, as a result, was court-martialed and imprisoned on Devil's Island. Later, because of irregularities during his trial, he was retried and then, though still found guilty, he was granted a pardon. Finally, after twelve years, he succeeded in proving his innocence, winning an appeal before the high court and gaining reinstatement in the army.

Although many non-Jews, like Emile Zola, believed in Dreyfus' innocence and worked to clear his name, the incident, nevertheless had obvious anti-Semitic overtones. When Dreyfus was stripped of his rank and disgraced out of the National Military Academy, he was greeted by clenched-fist crowds screaming, *"a bas les Juifs,"* meaning *"down with the Jews."* For many Jews in Europe during the nineteenth century, the scene confirmed their growing belief that anti-Semitism would never disappear and that the Jews would never become full-fledged citizens of Europe.

One of the advocates of this point of view was Theodor Herzl, a Hungarian-born Jewish writer and journalist, who is regarded as one of the greatest influences in the movement that led to the creation of the state of Israel. In fact, Herzl is credited as the founder of modern political Zionism. In February 1896, he published *Der Judenstaat,* translated as *"The Jewish State,"* which soon became the manifesto of the emerging Zionist movement. Herzl was the first to call for immediate political and international recognized action. To help implement his plan he called for a Zionist congress, which met in Basel, Switzerland in 1897. As a result of the congress, Palestine was chosen as the site of the future state because of its association with Jewish history. The World Zionist Organization was also established to

Jewish Settlers in Palestine, c.1920

In response to European anti-Semitism during the 19th century, a Zionist congress chose Palestine as the location for a future Jewish home state as early as 1897. Although Israel was not established until 1948, Jewish settlers (like those seen here) experienced challenges from local Arab residents.

help lay the economic foundation for the proposed state.

Initially, Palestinian reaction to Jewish settlement and the purchase of land was sporadic and impulsive, but over time it became more conscious, political, and more sustained. The early responses consisted of individual attacks by Arab peasants who were deprived of their land by Jewish settlers. The first formally recorded act of Palestinian opposition was in the form of a telegram signed by several Palestinians, and sent from Jerusalem to Istanbul. It urged the Ottoman authorities to prohibit Russian Jews from entering Palestine and acquiring land. This is significant because most of the land obtained by Jewish settlers was purchased from two sources, the Ottoman government or large estate owners. Few Palestinian peasants sold their land, which they had long cultivated under the traditional land tenure system. Instead, they were either evicted or transformed into laborers on land they no longer had any control over. Thus began a process of dispossession and disillusionment that would erupt into violent confrontation time and time again.

When formal appeals to the authorities failed, unofficial opposition to Zionism began to express itself more spontaneously, directly and forcefully. Violent clashes between Palestinians and Jewish immigrants occurred in Jaffa, and Arabs attacked Jewish settlers in the district of Tabariyya. Aside from these physical confrontations, a steady stream of written appeals were sent to Ottoman authorities protesting the sale of land to Zionist settlers. Najib Nasser, the editor of Haifa's newspaper *al-Karmel,* was arrested for disturbing the peace because of the inflammatory nature of articles he had written opposing the sale of land to Zionist settlers. Although he was later acquitted of all charges, his attitude reflected the increasing fear, concern, and resentment that Palestinians experienced during the years before the First World War.

The sale and acquisition of land became a constant source of tension between these two competing groups. While the majority of Jewish immigrants clustered in Palestinian cities, some attempted to establish agricultural settlements. By 1908, these were twenty-six such colonies with ten thousand members on four hundred thousand *dumums* of land, an equivalent of one hundred thousand acres. Much of the land purchased in the early years was acquired by private individuals. Increasingly, however, larger estates were purchased by the Jewish Colonial Association, or JCA, and the Jewish National Fund, or the

JNF. These lands were held *"in trust"* for the Jewish people as a whole.

By 1910, Palestinian newspapers and the public at large raised a cry of outrage over the sale of land totaling twenty-four thousand dumums, approximately six thousand acres of land, between Nazareth and Jenin by a rich merchant by the name Emile Sursoq of Beirut. The land was purchased by the JCA. The governor of the Nazareth district attempted to prevent the exchange but failed. In 1913, the Sursoqs sold another twenty-two dumums in Marj Ibn 'Amer to the JCA, which displaced hundreds if not thousands of Arab families.

One of the earliest written documents in opposition to the Zionist movement was a book by Najib 'Azoury, a Christian Arab who had studied in France and then served in the Ottoman Administration in Jerusalem. His *Le Reveil de La Nation Arabe,* or *The Awakening of the Arab Nation,* called for the separation of Arab provinces from Ottoman rule and predicted violent clashes in Palestine between the Arabs and the Jews for control of the area. Specifically, he wrote that, "Two important phenomena, of identical character but nevertheless opposed, which till now have not attracted attention, are now making their appearance in Asian Turkey: these are the awakening of the Arab nation and the latent efforts of the Jews to re-establish, on an extremely large scale, the ancient kingdom of Israel. These two movements are destined to struggle continuously with one another, until one prevails over the other. The fate of the entire world depends on the result of this struggle between the two peoples, which represent two contradictory principles."

Loaves and Fishes, c. 1920

As Europe plunged into World War I, the Ottoman Empire began arresting both Arab and Zionist leaders, forcing peasants into military service. When the Empire finally collapsed in 1918, British colonial forces took control of a region that was now in a state of chaos.

4

Palestine and the British Mandate

The beginning of World War I on August 1, 1914, ended an extended period, if not of relative peace, then at least a period when the colonial powers of Europe had avoided outright warfare. Of course, there had been the Crimean War in the middle of the nineteenth century, but since the Franco-Russian war in 1870, and the Russo-Turkish war seven years later; peace through diplomacy had been the guiding principle that prevented the countries of Europe from plunging into the depths of catastrophe. Even so, many of the past grievances and resentments, many of the old rebuffs, and slaps at individual country's pride and integrity, continued to fester just beneath the surface of this strained diplomacy.

The French still hoped to avenge their defeat at the hands of the Prussians in 1870, and remained deeply suspicious of British colonial ambition not only in the Middle East, but in Africa as well. Russia continued to view Ottoman territories, especially Constantinople, with an acquisitive eye. Britain, still the dominant power, desired to maintain the status quo and hence the territorial integrity of the Ottoman Empire if for no other reason that this placed the Ottomans as a buffer and protector of territories of great strategic importance to Great Britain, such as southern Iraq and the Suez Canal, without challenge from other European powers.

However, in spite, of their mutual mistrust, Britain, France, and eventually Russia became allies in 1914. They established an *Entente Cordial,* or *"cordial understanding."* This diplomatic relationship, sometimes known as the *"Triple Entente"* or simply *"Entente"* reflected their fear of a common enemy more than a sincere trust of each other's motives. The common enemy in this case was Germany, whose industrial and military expansion since the 1880s, coupled with its global ambitions in regards to its acquisition of colonies, created a general concern among the other colonial powers. So much so, that Britain resolved its dispute with France over colonial territories in the common interest of restraining Germany. Likewise, Britain settled its outstanding conflicts with Russia.

Strictly from a British point of view, Germany had gained too many concessions from the Ottomans, which threatened British colonial interests. The most significant was the construction of a railway from Constantinople through southern Iraq to Basra and the Persian Gulf. British officials considered southern Iraq as a sphere of military and commercial influence, as well as part of a defense perimeter, protecting civilian and military personnel working in the oil fields of the Gulf and in southwest Iran.

Britain controlled these fields, which were vital to its military position in Europe and Asia. Beginning in 1912, the British navy ran strictly on oil, the majority of which came from the Middle East, particularly Iran. In addition, there was also evidence of large oil deposits in northern Iraq and Mosul that would prove vital to British economic and political stability. Therefore, these matters made the British government extremely nervous regarding any hint of Germany attempting to challenge their colonial domination. It is in this context of British strategic self-interest, often-times at the expense of the people of the region, that one can begin to analyze the nature of the promises and pledges made to the Arabs and Jewish settlers during the course of World War I and its aftermath, and understand how these radically transformed the nature and future of the Middle East.

Caught like pawns in this international game of seek and destroy, the population of Palestine suffered immensely during the carnage of the first World War. The Ottomans arrested both Arab nationalists and Zionist leaders. They executed many of their Arab prisoners and they gave the majority of the Jewish leaders a choice between prison or exile. As a result, Arab protest in Palestine became virtually nonexistent and Zionist leaders, most notable among them David Ben-Gurion, who later became Israel's first prime minister, and Yitzhak Ben-Zvi, went into exile. Furthermore, since Palestine was used as a military base for the Ottoman army, food was in short supply, crops and livestock were commandeered to feed hungry troops, and trees were cut down and used as a source of fuel. Also, thousands of Arab peasants were conscripted to serve in the military, which further added to the already heavy burdens the people of Palestine were forced to bear. As a result, by the time the Ottoman Empire collapsed and British forces took control of Palestine in the first half of 1918, the country was in a state of

Ben-Gurion, c. 1956

David Ben-Gurion, who would later become Israel's first Prime Minister, was among those arrested by the Ottoman forces during World War I.

chaos and anarchy. Many people were on the brink of starvation and hunger was rampant throughout the country-side as well as in the urban areas. Thus, in the Middle East, particularly in Palestine, World War I was a crucial event that, along with the collapse of the Ottoman Empire, directed the twentieth-century destiny of the Arab world.

Starting in 1915, Britain entered into three separate agreements, with the French government, with Sharif Hussein of Mecca, who was the leader of the Arab revolt against the Ottoman authorities, and Lord Rothschild, who was the leader of the Zionist movement in Britain. These were the Sykes-Picot Agreement, the McMahon-Hussein Agreement, and the Balfour Declaration. All three of these agreements were to have explosive consequences for the Palestinian struggle for independence.

Although the Ottomans had a long- standing relationship with the British Empire, when World War I started they, nevertheless, aligned themselves with Germany against the Entente powers. As a result, during the war Britain encouraged the Arabs to revolt against the Ottomans and to join in the fighting on the side of Britain, France, and Russia. In return for Arab support in the war effort, they promised certain concessions. These promises resulted in a formal agreement between Hussein and Sir Henry McMahon, the British high commissioner.

Specifically, the British promised to support Arab independence in exchange for their allegiance during the war. Hussein and McMahon exchanged eight letters in which their agreements were specified. For example, in a letter to Hussein, written on October 24, 1915, McMahon wrote that, "Great Britain is prepared to recognize and support the independence of the Arabs in all the regions within all the limits demanded by the Sharif of Mecca." Hussein and other Arab representatives viewed this agreement as the basis for a united Arab kingdom in the former domains of the Ottoman Empire, including Palestine. In keeping with this agreement they rendered valuable assistance to the British by seizing the port of Aqaba, which made it possible to attack Ottoman forces in Palestine from the southeast, as well as Egypt. They also prevented the Germans from establishing a submarine base in the Red Sea.

In the meantime, the British entered into an agreement with the French government, known as the Sykes-Picot Agreement. This negotiated settlement provided for the division of the former Ottoman territories between Britain and France. Under this arrangement France was to have authority in coastal and northern regions of Syria, and Britain would control Iraq, Transjordan, and the port cities of Haifa and Acre. Palestine was to be placed under an international administration consisting of the "Triple Entente" and representatives of the Sharif of Mecca. This arrangement blatantly contradicted the agreement the British had made with the Arabs almost a year earlier.

To make matters even more complicated was the Balfour Declaration of November 1917, which expressed a desire to further Jewish aspirations in Palestine at the conclusion of the war. This third, and final agreement was delivered in the form of a letter from Lord Balfour, the British foreign secretary, to Lord Rothschild, leader of the Zionist movement in Britain. The tone of the letter is very explicit:

November 2, 1917

Dear Lord Rothschild,

I have much pleasure in conveying to you, on behalf of His Majesty's Government, the following declaration of sympathy with Jewish Zionist aspirations which has been submitted to, and approved by, the Cabinet. "His Majesty's Government view with favor the establishment in Palestine of a national home for the Jewish people, and will use their best endeavors to facilitate the achievement of this object, it being clearly understood that nothing shall be done which may prejudice the civil and religious rights of existing non-Jewish communities in Palestine, or in any other country." I should be grateful if you would bring this declaration to the knowledge of the Zionist Federation.

Yours sincerely,

Arthur James Balfour

These three contradictory agreements, and the British strategic interest that resulted because of them, set the stage for postwar conflicts between increased Arab Nationalism and Zionist's aspirations in regards to Palestine. Arab and Palestinian discontent erupted into demonstrations in Damascus, Haifa, Baghdad, Jaffa, and Jerusalem during the months of February, March, and April of 1920. In Palestine, escalating Palestinian and Zionist conflicts exploded into demonstrations and rioting during the festival of *Nebi Musa,* or *"Prophet Moses,"* a celebration that coincided with Passover and Easter. Four Arabs and five Jews were killed, and nearly three hundred people were wounded.

The British Commission of Inquiry, appointed to investigate the riots and their aftermath, submitted its report on July 1, 1920. It "listed as the causes of unrest in the country: British promises to Arabs during the war. The conflict between these promises and the Balfour Declaration, fear of Jewish domination, Zionist over-aggressiveness, and foreign propaganda."

In spite of the conclusions drawn by the commission, the British government, headed by Prime Minister David Lloyd George, continued to support Zionist aspirations outlined in the Balfour Declaration. On June 30, 1920, Lloyd George appointed Herbert Samuel, a British Zionist, as the first civilian high commissioner of Palestine. To no one's surprise, he was favorable to the building of a Jewish national home in the Holy Land.

A Caravan of Palestinian Police Cross the Desert on Camelback

Controlled first by the Ottoman Empire, and later by the British, Palestine's Arab residents began to resist colonial authority. The creation of Israel in 1948 solidified nationalist, anti-Zionist feelings among Arab Palestinians.

5

Palestinian Resistance to Israeli Occupation

*P*alestine first came under British control in December 1917, during the war with the Ottoman Empire. Invading from the Egyptian Sinai, British troops under General Edmund Allenby conquered Palestine and established a military administration that was called the *"Occupied Enemy Territory Administration,"* or "OETA." Ironically, it was with Arab and Palestinian military support that made it possible for the British to defeat the Ottomans in Palestine. It was also with Arab and Palestinian support that made it possible for the British to successfully set up a military administration in Palestine. Of course, as we have seen, this support came at a high cost for the people of the Middle East and was the result of their faith in

British promises that, "Great Britain was prepared to recognize the independence of the Arabs in all the regions within all the limits demanded by the Sharif of Mecca." This miscalculated faith in British promises would cost years of turmoil and thousands upon thousands of Arab lives. The British OETA lasted for thirty months, until June 30, 1920, when it was replaced by a civilian administration headed by Herbert Samuel.

The military administration was bound by and attempted to rule Palestine in accordance with international law, particularly, the *Manual of Military Law*. This manual was the product of the Hague Conferences of 1899 and 1907, two international conventions, which were organized for the purpose of bringing together the principal nations of the world to discuss and resolve the problems of maintaining universal peace, reducing armaments, and alleviating the conditions of warfare. Of equal importance for the people of Palestine was the fact that the *Manual of Military Law* obligated *"conquering armies,"* in this case the British military, to maintain the status quo of conquered territories until their future had been determined. As a result, the establishment of a Jewish national home was not a top priority for the British Military Administration of Palestine, especially when confronted with the devastation caused by the war. Another factor that had to be taken into consideration was Arab hostility toward Zionism, which was inspired both by awareness of the Balfour Declaration and the actions and attitudes of Zionist who demanded an immediate creation of a Jewish State. Although these were vital issues that could not be ignored, at the same time, there were other, more urgent concerns.

Because Palestine had served as a staging area for Ottoman troops throughout much of the war, and finally as a battleground, the Ottomans had conscripted thousands of Arab peasants and confiscated their crops. There was extensive deforestation because entire forests had been utilized for fuel in the war effort. These developments coupled with locust plagues, poor harvests due to bad weather and labor shortages in the villages, contributed to an overall sense of chaos and despair. Starvation and disease of famine proportion spread throughout the cities, especially among the poorer inhabitants, but basically, no one was spared, Christian, Jew, or Muslim. Therefore, faced with the enormity of these problems, the immediate task of the British military administration was to provide food and medical supplies to the people in need and to restore a sense of social and economic order. This was the sense of order they had helped to destroy with their long tradition of strategic self-interest and intervention in the region.

The British military administration's policy of maintaining the status quo and of addressing the more urgent needs of the region, put them on a collision course with Zionist leaders who were anxious to get down to the business of creating a Jewish state. Although the Zionists had the support of the British Foreign Office, nevertheless, the OETA policy was upheld the majority of the time.

For the time being it appeared that the British had found a temporary stalemate to the impending crisis. But this momentary solution was not a permanent answer to Zionist requests to participate in the military administration of the country, a creation of a land authority, which would include Jewish experts to survey the region's resources, and the formation of an exclusively Jewish military force. And it certainly did nothing to appease Arab hostility and resentment toward Zionist aspirations, as was aptly pointed out by a member of the OETA, "The antagonism to Zionism of the majority of the population is deep-rooted, it is fast leading to hatred of the British, and will result, if the Zionist program is forced upon them, in an outbreak of serious character."

In an effort to find a longer-lasting solution to the region's problems the King-Crane Commission was established in 1919. Known for the names of its two members, Henry C. King, president of Oberlin College and Charles Crane, a Chicago businessman, the commission was empowered, at the suggestion of President Woodrow Wilson, to provide an unbiased report of the wishes of the Palestinian and Arab people in regards to their future. It reported that Arab wishes "were nationalistic, that is to say they called for a united Syria, including Lebanon and Palestine, under a democratic constitution, making no distinction on the basis of religion."

Based on its findings, the commission recommended independence for Syria and Palestine or, failing that, a mandate under the United States, not Britain, in accordance with the wishes of the Arab people. In regards to Zionist aspirations, the commission recommended "serious modification of the extreme Zionist Program."

Although the King-Crane Commission had been established in cooperation with the Allied powers, Britain, France, Russia, and the United States, its findings were virtually ignored. In fact, the report was not published until 1922, three years after it was written, but more importantly, a full two years after the future of Palestine and the Palestinians had been determined at the Conference of San Remo.

Beginning on April 19, 1920, and lasting six days, an international conference was convened at San Remo, on the Italian Riviera. The purpose of the conference was to decide the future of the former territories of the Ottoman Turkish Empire. It was attended by the prime ministers of Great Britain, France, and Italy with representatives from Japan, Greece, and Belgium. The conference approved the final framework of a peace treaty that abolished the Ottoman

San Remo Conference, May 13, 1920

In 1920, an international conference was convened at San Remo on the Italian Riviera. Designed to decide the future of former German and Ottoman territories, the conference was attended by leaders from the victorious European nations and, among its determinations, decided to grant control of Palestine to Great Britain.

Empire, obligated the former empire to renounce all rights over Arab Asia and North Africa.

During the conference of San Remo, several "mandates" were created out of the Ottoman territories in the Middle East. A *"mandate,"* was a term used to describe the administration of territories formerly held by Germany and the Ottoman Empire. The territories were placed under the supervision of the League of Nations, and the administration of the mandates was delegated to the victorious powers until the areas could govern themselves.

Two mandates were created out of the old Ottoman province of Syria. The northern half, which consisted of Syria and Lebanon, was mandated to France. The southern half, which consisted solely of Palestine, was mandated to Great Britain. Iraq was also mandated to Britain. An Anglo-French oil agreement was also concluded at San Remo, providing France with a twenty-five percent share of the oil shipped from the oil fields of Iraq. In exchange the French agreed not to challenge British claims to Mosul.

From this point forward, the fate of Palestine and the Palestinians was sealed as far as European intervention was concerned. Although the stated purpose of the mandatory system was to promote the well-being and development of the indigenous population, many critics of the system believed that it was nothing more than a thinly disguised opportunity for the victorious nations to promote their own political, economic, and strategic self-interest. For example, the text of the British Mandate in regards to Palestine, incorporated the Balfour Declaration. The text also contained language giving explicit recognition "to the historical connection of the Jewish people with Palestine and the grounds for reconstituting their national home in that country. Among other references written into the text of the mandatory document was a provision stating that "The Administration of Palestine shall facilitate Jewish immigration under suitable conditions and shall encourage close settlement by Jews on the land, including state lands and waste lands not required for public purposes."

While Zionists were pleased with the mandate provisions, Palestinians were increasingly alarmed because, whereas numerous references were made about the *"Jewish Community,"* Arabs and Palestinians, who constituted ninety percent of the population, were referred to, over and over again, merely as *"the other section"* of the population. At the same time, another example that Britain was pursuing its own self-interest, was that the overall postwar settlement conformed much too closely to the arrangement set forth in the secret Sykes-Picot agreement of 1916. The French had obtained their strategic objectives with their possession of Syria and Lebanon, and the British were in control of the territories they deemed essential for the protection of their self-interests. Compared to Iraq, which had an unlimited supply of oil, Palestine was a poor country lacking in resources, investment, and growth potential. Nevertheless, it was of strategic importance to the British strategic schemes in the Middle East. The country was the primary buffer state in Great Britain's defense of India, Egypt, and the Suez Canal, which was the shortest sea route to India. Palestine was also part of the air routes to India and Iraq, but more importantly the country served as a primary terminus of the oil pipelines from the Iraqi oil fields, which were operated by the British-owned Iraq Petroleum Company, or IPC.

Furthermore, the Jewish presence in Palestine seemed likely to prevent the country from evolving into an independent Arab state, which was the prime objective of the Mandatory System and at the same time, it gave England extensive powers, virtually life and death decisions, over the people of the region. These included legislative and administrative authority and responsibility for Palestine's foreign relations, domestic security and defense. They also provided that the mandatory power shall be entitled at all times to use the roads, railways and ports of Palestine for the movement of armed forces and the carriage of fuels and supplies.

Political activity surrounding the establishment of the mandatory system involved questions of who would control the former Ottoman Territories and in Palestine, to what degree would the political rights asserted by Arabs and Jews be respected. Increasingly, Palestinians found themselves in a position of being disenfranchised, dispossessed of their dreams of independence and subjugated to the rules and regulations of British strategic self-interest. Even though they were the majority, no Arab was nominated to be the head of a government post. The percentage of their representation in government was less than the ratio of their size to total population. Furthermore, their inclusion was designed to *"emasculate Arab nationalist opposition to the mandatory system,"* while excluding them from positions in which they might be able to exert influence against that system. Typically, when a qualified Arab was given a position of responsibility, it was only after British officials decided to save money, because they could always pay Arab personnel a lower salary.

As far as the mandatory system was concerned, circumstances for Jews were quite the opposite. They were not subjected to the same personal or economic disadvantages. Their salaries were higher, and their participation was a means of furthering Zionist objectives, which they advocated. And in situations in which British officials had made important decisions regarding issues important to the Jewish community, they could often rely on an official who was at least sympathetic to the Zionist cause, if not a committed member of the movement.

As the mandatory system became more pronounced, Palestinians and Arabs found themselves in a position of being written out of their own history, reduced in status from the majority population of Palestine to that of *"the other section"* of the population. These developments set the stage from which Arab and Zionist conflict was to evolve in Palestine during the years between the two world wars.

British Troops Patrolling the Streets of Jerusalem, c. Early 20th Century

Between the World Wars, Palestinian discontent with British rule began to grow. Nationalist feelings among local Muslims were further fueled by waves of Jewish immigration, resulting in a state of unrest that forced Britain to fully occupy and police the country.

6

Palestinian Resistance to Dispossession

As previously stated, the first signs of Palestinian discontent with the British Administration of the region occurred in April 1920, during the celebration of the Nebi Musa festival. The disturbance was triggered by a confrontation between Palestinians and a procession of Jews. A British-appointed commission investigated the incident but no recommendations or findings were ever published. Riots also erupted during another celebration on May Day, 1921. Most of the Palestinian and Arab discontent that was expressed during this disturbance was in the aftermath of the conference of San Remo. This also led to political tension not only in Palestine, but Syria, Lebanon, and Iraq as well.

The renewal of Jewish immigration following the conference at

San Remo also inflamed tensions between the Arab and Jewish communities. Palestinians perceived the arrival of ten thousand Jewish immigrants between December 1920 and April 1921 as a terrible omen of what the future would bring if something substantial was not done.

In May 1921, a rebellion erupted in Iraq and lasted throughout the summer, followed by disturbances in several other cities. Forty-seven Jews and forty-eight Arabs were killed. Two hundred and fourteen people were wounded. Numerous Palestinians were killed by British in their efforts to defend Jewish settlements.

Arabs and Palestinians also tried more peaceful and diplomatic ways of addressing their problems. In August 1921, a delegation, led by Musa Kazim al-Husayni, carried their protests to London. The delegation included both Muslims and Christians. It spent nearly a year negotiating with the British and even visited the League of Nations in Geneva, Switzerland, to protest the plight of the Palestinians and Arabs in general. Their one unyielding demand was that the Balfour Declaration be rescinded. The group presented their arguments in a booklet titled, *The Holy Land: The Moslem-Christian Case Against Zionist Aggression.*

In response to the delegation's diplomatic efforts, the British made it clear to the Palestinians that the Balfour Declaration would continue to be a guiding principle directing British efforts to govern the region and the people who lived there. However, they did encourage further discussion regarding "The real fear with which the Arabs regarded the idea of Jewish immigration," and "the real fear" with which they regarded the Jewish sudden rise to political power in Palestine following the war and the conference at San Remo.

In February 1922, Winston Churchill, who was then colonial secretary, presented the Palestinian delegation with a draft of the constitution that Herbert Samuel had promised the previous summer. This new constitution stated that the future British Mandate government in Palestine would consist of a legislative council composed of the high commissioner, ten appointed British officials, and fifteen local representatives. Nine of these representatives would be Muslim, three Christian, and three Jewish. In response, the delegation rejected the constitution, stating that they would not discuss any constitutional arrangements as long as the Balfour Declaration was still intact.

Under growing pressure, the British issued a *"white paper,"* or the draft of another proposal, which would provide an official interpretation of the Balfour Declaration, and would also clarify British policy toward Jewish immigration in a manner acceptable not only to the members of the delegation but also to mainstream Arab opinion. The white paper was also presented to members of the World Zionist Organization, who responded favorably. The Palestinian delegation, on the other hand, flatly rejected the document, stating that its endorsement of the principles of the Balfour Declaration made it unacceptable, in spite of some provisions that addressed Arab concerns. Nevertheless, despite the delegation's response, Churchill signed the document, and it was approved by the British parliament early in July 1922. It provided Great Britain's official interpretation of the British Mandate in Palestine, pending the formal adoption of the League of Nations.

In particular, the Palestinian delegation opposed the white paper because it affirmed that Jews were in Palestine "as a right and not on sufferance," which meant that the Jewish claim to Palestine was as valid as the Palestinian claim, and that they did not require the sanction or permission of the Palestinian people in order to occupy territory within the region. But, what was even more crucial, as far as the Palestinian position was concerned, was the assertion that "the existence of a Jewish National Home in Palestine should be internationally guaranteed," and "formally recognized to rest upon ancient historic connection." This new interpretation completely, from the standpoint of British policy, undermined the idea of Palestinian authority in the region. Once again, by intent or accident, British intervention had served the cause of reducing the status of the indigenous population of Palestine and casting them permanently in the role of the *"other,"* more specifically, "the other section of the population."

Although their efforts in Britain had been frustrated, Palestinian people continued to search for effective means to exercise their rights as a free and independent people, and to express their discontent and resentment when these rights were denied. Of all of their frustrations, the two most important issues to emerge or reemerge in the aftermath of World War I and the British Mandate were Jewish immigration and the acquisition of land.

In regard to the first important issue, Palestine in 1882 had a small, national Jewish community, or *"Yishuv"* as Israeli and western Jewish historians call it. At that point the total Jewish population was approximately twenty-four thousand compared to roughly five hundred thousand Palestinians. The size of the Jewish community increased in Palestine from 1882, through several distinct periods of immigration called *"aliyahs."* The *"first wave,"* approximately twenty-five thousand immigrants, arrived between 1882 and 1903, the majority were fleeing the pogroms in Russia. The *"second wave,"* or aliyahs, arrived between 1904 and 1914, on the eve of World War I. About thirty-five thousand people arrived in Palestine during this period, and they were mostly from Eastern Europe. By the end of this second phase of immigration the total Jewish population of Palestine was eighty-five thousand.

The end of the First World War marked the beginning of the *"third wave"* of Jewish immigration. This continued between 1919 and 1923, and brought in approximately thirty-five thousand immigrants, most of who were from Russia. The *"fourth wave,"* between 1924 and 1931 brought approximately eighty-five thousand immigrants, mostly of Polish origin and middle-class background. The fifth and final phase of Jewish immigration occurred between 1932 and 1938, and is estimated to be close to two hundred thousand individuals. This dramatic increase is due to the rise of Nazism in Germany and other parts of Europe. This heavy influx raised the Jewish population in Palestine to an estimated three hundred and seventy thousand people, approximately twenty-eight percent of the total population. This is a dramatic increase, especially when you take into consideration that the December 1931 census of Palestine showed that of the one million four hundred thousand people, eighty-four percent were Arab and sixteen percent were Jewish. Based on these figures, the Jewish population had nearly doubled in less than five years. In fact, of the two hundred thousand that had entered Palestine during the *"fifth wave,"* a hundred and seventy-four thousand had arrived during the four years between 1932 and 1936.

Given these developments it is not surprising that the Palestinian population became increasingly alarmed at the staggering rise in the Jewish settlers living in Palestine and the surrounding region. In a very short span of time the cultural, political, and economic composition was completely altered, and all without the consent and against the will of the Palestinian people. This radical change, especially during the years between 1932 and 1936, without a doubt fueled Palestinian discontent and resentment toward Jewish immigration. It would not be long before these feelings of frustration erupted into open rebellion. But immigration was not the only cause that created conflict between Palestine's two diametrically opposed communities.

This, then, brings us to the second significant issue, which frustrated Palestinian hopes and dreams of an independent, self-governing, Palestinian nation. And that is the issue of land acquisition. Despite the often-quoted Zionist point of view that Palestine was a land without people, the Jewish immigrants, upon their arrival, discovered that Palestinian land was not uninhabited or readily available. It has been suggested that as far as Zionist aspirations in regards to Palestine were concerned, land purchase and immigration complemented one another in pursuit of the goal of creating a Jewish majority in as many districts as possible. Therefore, the first priority in the selection of land for purchase was how it could be used to attain and sustain a Jewish majority. This was important to Zionist aspirations because, should the day come when Palestine would be divided among Arab and Jewish inhabitants, which is precisely what was proposed by commissions of inquiry investigating later disturbances, land holdings might well determine the extent and location of territory allocated to Jews. As a result of Zionist land acquisition, thousands of Arabs who worked the land for livelihood were forced to leave. Like two trains traveling at uncontrolled speed along the same tracks, from opposite directions, the Arab and Jewish communities were headed toward a terrible catastrophe.

While peasants and the urban poor rioted and used violence against Jewish settlers, but not yet against British authorities, the Palestinian people in towns and villages organized themselves into Muslim-Christian associations, Arab Literary clubs, the Higher Islamic Council, and other groups in a national effort to resist Zionist aspirations. The Palestinian elite launched a campaign, which they hoped would influence British policy. The "Palestine Arab Congress," which claimed to represent "all classes and creeds of the Arab people of Palestine," was held in Haifa and elected twenty-two members called the Palestine Arab Executive. It joined the top leaders of the two competing notable Arab families of Jerusalem, the "Husseinis," and the "Nashashibis." The political platform of this movement included the condemnation of the Balfour Declaration, and the idea of a Jewish national home in Palestine, as well as the mandate's support of it. The political platform also rejected the idea of mass Jewish immigration into Palestine, but advocated for the establishment of a national government in Palestine. This last point was significant because Palestine, like Syria, and Iraq, was designated by the League of Nations to establish a national government with legislative and administrative structures.

Although the Palestine Arab Executive movement united the rival political clans of the Husseinis and the Nashashibis in an organization that spoke for all Palestinians, the internal rivalry, which developed within the group actually intensified and served as a means to sabotage the unity of the group as well as the Palestinian struggle against the Zionist and the British. The deciding factor came when al-Hajj Amin al-Husseini was appointed *"mufti,"* or "legal advisor," by Herbert Samuel instead of the Nashashibi candidate. Al-Hajj Amin was also elected president of the "Supreme Muslims Council" over his Nashashibi rival. This was an important position because al-Hajj Amin was in charge of the communities financial resources, the *Shari'a,* or Muslim law courts, as well as schools, orphanages, mosques, and other institutions to which he held to the power to appoint and dismiss employees. He expanded welfare and health clinics, built an orphanage, renovated and supported schools, and organized a tree-planting program. Most symbolic, however was that he restored two mosques, the al-Aqsa and the Dome of the Rock, on the al-Haram al Sharif in Jerusalem through an international Muslim fund-raising campaign.

Al-Hajj Amin Effendi al-Husseini, c. 1938

In the face of fading hopes for an independent, self-governing Palestine, Haj Amin al-Husseini (seen here) was elected president of the "Supreme Muslims Council." Although he initiated many social programs and restored several historic mosques, al-Husseini was unable to reconcile rival Arab factions in the region.

In spite of these achievements the rivalry between the Husseinis and the Nashashibis still continued. In fact, the Nashashibis attempted to form an opposing power base in the form of the National Party, and encouraged the creation of peasant parties. The National Party distanced themselves from the Palestine Arab Executive by arguing for greater cooperation with the British authorities. They pointed out that opposition to the British Mandate had failed to bring about the desired changes or even slightly alter British policy in the region, therefore, it only seemed reasonable, from their vantage point, to work within the system rather than trying to direct change through opposition. These political developments both reflected and fueled the bitter rivalry between the two nationalist factions, which in turn kept the Palestinians from achieving their larger political goals. This divisiveness would result in dire consequences in the decade to come.

Aerial View of old Jaffa, c. 1988

Increased Jewish immigration and British occupation during the first half of the 20th century put a strain on Palestine's resources and people. Feeling dispossessed and disenfranchised, Palestine's peasant Arab population began to take a more radical and violent stance.

7

The Arab Revolt

*U*nlike the Palestinian elite, who attempted more traditional methods of resistance, the peasant parties or groups were more radical in their approach. For this reason they were often seen as the vanguard of the violent struggle, first against the Zionist, and later on, against the British authorities. The leaders of the peasant groups, as well as the ordinary rank and file members, even more than their elite counterparts, demanded immediate social and economic relief from the worsening conditions brought about by Jewish immigration and land acquisition, and other Zionist aspirations in regards to Palestine. More so than the elite politicians and the Palestinian notables, it was the Palestinian peasants and the urban poor who bore the brunt of this onslaught. And, in more than just a symbolic or figurative sense, their backs were against the wall once they had lost their land, their homes, and their place in the social order. They had little else to lose. This overwhelming sense of dispossession and disenfranchisement contributed to the increasingly radical and confrontational mood of the Palestinians. Over time, as other more traditional means failed, this mood began to spread throughout other areas of Arab society.

Although violent confrontation had largely subsided after the rebellions of the early 1920s, a combination of factors, some that we have already discussed including Jewish immigration and land purchases, but also economic conditions for Palestinians, including unemployment and impoverishment of the urban poor, created a highly charged and politically explosive situation.

Matters came to a head on Friday, August 23, 1929. A confrontation between Arabs and Jews erupted into a virtual bloodbath in which nearly two hundred and fifty people were killed and almost twice that many were wounded. Fueled by wild rumors and accusations the violence erupted in Jerusalem and spread to several other cities such as Haifa, Jaffa, Safad, and Hebron. It was finally suppressed by the British after a week of turmoil.

The British response was to create another commission, the Shaw Commission, to study the causes of the disturbances. The administration also created a second commission, the Hope-Simpson Commission, to conduct a thorough study of the social and economic conditions in the country. The Shaw Commission, published March 1930, concluded that the basic cause of the disturbances was the Palestinian people's feeling "of disappointment of their political and national aspirations and fear for their economic future."

In particular, it identified Zionist immigration and land practices as the primary reasons for the 1929 outbreaks. It declared that "a landless and discontented class is being created," and called for limitations on the transfer of land to non-Arabs.

In the meantime, the Hope-Simpson Commission, headed by Sir John Hope-Simpson, issued the *Passfield White Paper,* on May 27, 1930, that reaffirmed the conclusions reported by the Shaw Commission. In it, Lord Passfield and his report came under vigorous attack by the Zionist and pro-Zionist in Britain and Palestine. This political pressure overwhelmed the minority government of the new British Prime Minister Ramsay MacDonald. In response to this political pressure MacDonald wrote a letter that in effect repudiated and reversed the policy recommendations outlined in the Passfield report. This policy reversal kept in place the exact social, economic, political, and institutional processes that the British administration had determined to be the causes of disturbances in Palestine. For many Palestinians, especially those who straddled the fence that separated traditional methods of protest from more radical and violent means, this confirmed how much power and influence the Zionists exercised over the British government. For a long time now, more radical Arabs had advocated armed resistance, not only against the Zionists but against the British authorities as well. Now, in the aftermath of one final rejection, that did not seem like such a far-fetched idea. Whether the British knew it or not, they had set in motion what history would remember as *"The Arab Revolt."*

Several important incidents, in 1933, and 1935, contributed to the increasingly radical and confrontational mood of the Palestinians. On January 30, 1933, Adolf Hitler was sworn in as chancellor of Germany. He immediately passed laws that prevented Jewish participation in professional and commercial activities. The Nuremberg laws restricted citizenship to "Aryans" and banned marriage between Germans and Jews. Because of this rise in anti-Semitism, which was promoted and enforced by the German Government, German Jewish immigration increased dramatically. However, a majority of those leaving did not go directly to Palestine. Those who did were able to transfer much of their money, thanks to an arrangement made between Zionist leaders and the Nazi government. In fact, the Nazis were anxious to get rid of their so-called Jewish problem. So much so that they granted permission to the Zionist organization to establish training camps in Germany to prepare immigrants for their futures in Palestine. The SS officer in charge of making these arrangements was Adolf Eichman, who would later be responsible for the murder of millions of Jews during World War II.

German Jewish immigration to Palestine coincided with increased Jewish immigration from Eastern Europe, especially Poland. As previously discussed, between 1932 and 1936, during the *"fifth wave,"* the Jewish population in Palestine doubled. This influx, far more middle class than working class in composition, brought a major infusing of capital into Palestine, whose urban and Jewish sectors underwent an economic boom in the mid-1930s despite the worldwide depression. For the Arab population in Palestine, this new flood of immigrants was like pouring salt into old wounds.

The drastic increase in Jewish immigration was just one of the incidents that inflamed the already explosive tensions that existed between the Palestinian and Zionist communities. Another was the discovery of a shipment of guns that had been smuggled into the country. Palestinians believed that the shipment had been arranged by Jewish

agents. Whether this was true or not, the incident intensified Arab anger and frustration. The same year, 1935,
Sheikh Izz al-Din al-Qassam and several of his col-
laborators were killed by the police. Al-Qassam was
president of the Haifa branch of the Young Men's
Muslim Association. He devoted himself to organizing
young Arabs for direct action against the Zionist and
British authorities. His death made him a martyr to the
cause of militant nationalism.

As a leader, al-Qassam was significant because he
aligned himself with the rural peasantry, the urban poor,
and the displaced and landless peasants. His movement
was inspired by al-Qassam's concern for social justice
and his belief in direct confrontation. Although he was
a religious cleric, al-Qassam demanded that the mufti
provide money for arms, instead of building and
renovating mosques. He believed that the diplomatic
and political tactics used by the elite leadership was not
only ineffective in obtaining Palestinian rights but also
brought the country to the brink of disaster. Al-Qassam
was not the only Arab leader that held this view.
Numerous pan-Arabists (unity of all people of Arab
origin) and nationalist groups, including the Istiqlal
(Independence) Party, were critical of the moderate
Palestinian leadership and its diplomatic methods. The
leaders of these new, militant groups were articulate
men like Awni 'Abdul-Hadi', Akram Zu'ayter, Izzat
Darwaza, and Ahmad al-Shugayri, who later became the
first chairman of the Palestine Liberation Organization,
or PLO, in 1964. They advocated not only strong opposition to the Zionists but, more importantly, to the British
and the Mandate governments. They called for the
dismantlement of the British Mandate and its replacement
with Palestine Arab government. Such views captured
the imagination of the dispossessed and disenfranchised.

Following the death of al-Qassam, a large number of young Palestinians formed groups, and called themselves *Ikhwan al-Qassam,* or "Brothers of al-Qassam." They launched an armed struggle against both the Jewish settlers and the British authorities.

On April 15, 1936, members of the Ikhwan al-Qassam ambushed a bus and two Jewish passengers were killed. In retaliation a Jewish militia, *the Haganah,* or "Defense," killed two Palestinians. More counterattacks and reprisals followed, until the British declared a state of emergency. In response, on April 19, 1936, leaders of the Istiqlal and other nationalist groups announced a general strike that spread throughout the country. Part of what made the strike successful is that it involved middle-class businessmen and professionals in positions of leadership.

Support for the strike came from many different quarters. It was endorsed by eighteen mayors, petitions were also submitted by hundreds of senior and mid-level civil servants, and thousand of workers left their jobs, causing hundreds of businesses to close. As the strike gained momentum, the six existing Palestinian parties, including many members of the political elite, formed to coordinate strike activities. This body had ten members and was known as the *"al-Lajnah al-Arabiyya al-Ulya,"* or the *"Arab Higher Committee."*

The mufti, al-Hajj Amin al-Husseini was chosen to serve as president. Although serving in this capacity jeopardized his position with the British, since they were the ones who had appointed him to political office, he had few alternatives other than joining the militants. The Arab Higher Committee, or AHC, represented all political factions and social sections of Palestine society and advocated the complete end of Jewish immigration, and the prohibition of land sales to non-Arabs, and finally, the establishment of a national government responsible

Haganah troops, Palestine, c. 1948

In response to Arab attacks on Jewish settlers and British authorities in the 1930s, Palestinian Jews formed a militia called the *Haganah* (meaning "Defense") and began to fight back.

to a parliamentary or representative council.

The strike lasted six months. To provide food and other necessities for the strikers, the National Strike Committee operated special distribution centers. Workers also closed the port of Jaffa, and the Supreme Muslims Council closed its school. It was a well-organized and effective act of civil disobedience, but it was not long before civil disobedience turned into armed insurrection. A May Day demonstration in Haifa erupted into a violent confrontation when numerous demonstrators attacked the police, who responded by firing into the crowd. Several people were killed or wounded. Triggered by these deaths, the revolt spread into the countryside. Many peasant families contributed men, food, money, and shelter.

The rebels organized themselves into guerrilla bands *"fasa'il"* of a few men with a leader *"qa'id."* Guerrillas used hit-and-run tactics, primarily at night and usually in local areas that were familiar to them. As the revolt progressed, they operated on a regional or national command structure, especially after the arrival of Fawzi al-Qawuqji, a Syrian military leader, who would also serve in the crucial 1947-1948 conflict. It was the role of the guerrilla bands to be spontaneous and effective, an act they called *"Faz'a."* Faz'a was used in coming to the aid of other guerrilla bands, or forces under fire by British troops. Sometimes it was simply used for sounding the alarm, to alert fellow co-conspirators when British troops were on the move, similar to Paul Revere during America's war of independence. Also similar to American revolutionaries, the local guerrilla bands had the advantage of their small numbers and knowledge of the terrain to escape the British and hide among their kin people and fellow villagers.

The general strike formally ended in October 1936,

but the country by this time had been plunged into a prolonged period of violent confrontation. It is worthy to note that this period became widely known as The Arab Revolt and continued on an intermittent basis until it was interrupted by the beginning of World War II, in 1939. At the conclusion of the Second World War the conflict resumed and continued in one manifestation or another until the present day.

Arab Officials Meet and Reject the British Request to Allow More Jewish Immigration, c. 1946

Arab leaders saw Jewish immigration as the chief threat to their security, and called on British authorities to close the borders to further immigrants. When this request was denied, Arab workers began a series of crippling labor strikes.

8

The Beginning of the End

Both the strike and the armed insurrection that followed were not only a direct challenge to Zionist aspirations in Palestine, but also to British authority. This marked a turning point in the Palestinian struggle for independence. The significance of which was not lost on the British. In fact, to counter the revolt, the high commissioner quickly initiated a series of harsh, emergency regulations. Although these measures were designed to calm the tensions caused by the conflict, all they succeeded in doing was to further influence Arab resentment and hostility.

At that point the British declared the strike illegal, and in late September 1936, after the assassination of a British district commissioner, the British administration arrested, incarcerated, or deported strike leaders, and other prominent members of the Arab Higher Committee. They also censored or closed down newspapers, imposed strict curfews, and meted out harsh punishment to anyone remotely suspected of involvement in militant activities. They also conducted, without warrants, house-to-house search and seizure operations in an effort to disarm and intimidate Palestinian citizens, hoping that the tactics would quell the disturbances.

These disturbances also gave birth to another British commission of inquiry. The Palestine Royal Commission, sometimes known as the Peel Commission, was given the task of investigating the causes of the revolt and, at the same time, to explore ways and means of suppressing future Palestinian resistance. Under the direction of William Robert Wellesley, Lord Peel, the six-member Palestine Royal Commission began its investigation in November 1936 and eventually held sixty-six meetings, over thirty of them (in) secret. In July 1937, the commission published its report. It stated that the causes of the revolt were the same as those that had triggered rebellions in 1920, 1921, 1929, and 1933. Specifically, these causes were "the desire of the Arabs for national independence" and "their hatred and fear of the establishment of the Jewish National Home." The report then went on to elaborate that, "About 1,000,000 Arabs are in strife, open or latent, with 400,00 Jews. There is no common ground between them." Furthermore, the report stated, rather bluntly, that the British Mandate had not only failed to achieve its prime directive, it had deepened the antagonism between the two communities in Palestine. Therefore, it was the recommendation of the commission, that the Mandate should be ended and the territory of Palestine should be partitioned so that each "national community" would be able to guide its own destiny. This last proposal outraged the Palestinian community because they saw it as a means of dissecting their national homeland. But this was not the only repercussion of the recommendations issued by the Palestine Royal Commission.

Not long after the commission published its report, an order was issued for the arrest and detention of al-Hajj al-Husseini, who had served as president of the Arab Higher Committee. However, he was able to escape capture by crossing the border into Lebanon. The British also declared the Arab Higher Committee, and several other national organizations illegal. About the only Arab organization left in operation was the Nashashibis' National Defense Party, which deprived it of any credibility with the Arab community.

Even in spite of these setbacks the Arab revolt intensified following the Palestine Royal Commission's published report. It reached its climax during the summer of 1938. Numerous Palestinian cities, including Jerusalem, joined this most recent disturbance. In response, the British launched an all-out offensive to crush the uprising. They assembled two divisions of soldiers, squadrons of airplanes, the British police force in Palestine, the Transjordanian frontier forces, and six thousand Jewish auxiliaries. With these combined forces the British outnumbered the Palestinian rebels ten to one. Nevertheless, the conflict lasted until 1939, when the Palestinian people had fought to the end of their will and were finally overcome by weariness and exhaustion. But it was only after their leaders were in exile, and their fighting forces were surrounded and contained did the uprising subside into a terrifying and uneasy calm. But this was by no means the end of the struggle, just a brief respite.

During the calm that followed the terrible storm of insurrection, the British issued a white paper that, for the first time during the mandate, reversed its previous policy and made some substantial concessions to Palestinian concerns. Jewish immigration was limited to seventy-five thousand over a five-year period, land acquisition was restricted to limited areas, and Palestine would become independent within ten years if Arab-Jewish relations improved.

In response to these concessions, both the Arab rebels and the Zionists rejected the white paper proposals. Both felt that they had been short-changed by the British government. Nevertheless, despite its rejection by both communities, the British implemented the new plan. Because the British government was faced with a new world war, the white paper was seen as a quick solution to a deeply rooted problem. It would prove to be a miscalculation that the British would pay dearly for in the years to come. In the meantime the world was about to be plunged into war.

The Arab Revolt of 1936 had won for the Palestinian people many important concessions, but it failed to achieve its principal goal of immediate Palestinian independence. Throughout the next decade this aim would continue to be frustrated. Many crucial world events would be responsible for this growing sense of frustration and disillusionment. The Second World War, the Holocaust, the increased Jewish immigration, legal and illegal, from war-ravaged Europe to Palestine, and growing sympathy for European Jewry were all contributing factors in the demise of Palestinian dreams of self-determination. There were several factors that played a crucial role, including the increasing influence of the international Zionist movement, especially in the United States, coupled with the gradual decline of the British Empire, and the emergence of the United Nations. All of these elements combined to overwhelm Palestine and the Palestinians during the decade of the

Jews Disembark at Haifa Harbor Seeking Refuge in Palestine, c. 1946

Following World War II and the devastation of the Holocaust, even greater numbers of Jewish immigrants sought to start a new life in Palestine. Many, like those seen here, landed at Haifa harbor, hoping for a brighter future. Palestinian Arabs saw this as the end of any hope for Palestinian self-rule.

1940s. Although no one probably suspected it at the time, the country and its people were already on the road to al-Nakbah. In fact, the climax of Palestine's catastrophic destruction was just eight short years away.

During World War II, the Arabs of Palestine were disorganized and leaderless. In fact, the harsh suppression of the Palestinian Revolt decimated Palestinian political and military institutions. Nevertheless, Palestinians remained as determined as ever to derail Zionist aspirations. There were even some efforts to revitalize the Arab nationalist movement. But, for a variety of reasons, the forceful spirit that animated political activism and revolt in the 1930s did not return to full force during the war years.

In contrast, the Jewish community in the 1940s grew economically stronger, became tightly organized politically and militarily. With the aid of British training, the *Haganah* militia, the forces controlled by the Jewish Agency, and other defense militia grew in numbers, skill, and sophistication. In addition, two Jewish terrorist groups *Irgun* and the *Lohamei Herut Yisrel,* sometimes referred to as the Lehi and Stern Gang, also gained some prominence. Jewish military power was further increased by the experience and technical skill acquired by the thirty-seven thousand volunteers in the Jewish Brigade and other units who served in the British protection from the beginning of the mandate, the Jewish community by the end of the war became strong enough militarily to launch a revolt against the British in 1945, and the conquest of Palestine three years later. In other words, there was a decisive shift in the balance of power between the two opposing communities, the immigrant-settler Jewish community and the indigenous Palestinians. This shift would prove fateful.

In 1942, a year after the United States entered World War II, a Zionist conference was held at the Biltmore Hotel in New York City. During this conference a new Zionist program was announced. This marked a significant turning point in the Zionist struggle to further their aspirations in Palestine. Increasingly frustrated with Great Britain because strategic self-interest before and during World War II made it necessary to make substantial concessions to Arab states, the Zionists turned for support to the United States, the emerging world power. It was a fruitful moment for the

Zionists to air the case to the world because sympathy for the European Jews suffering brutal Nazi atrocities increased throughout the world. The conference at the Biltmore provided the Zionists and their cause an international forum. In opposition to the 1939 British White Paper, they demanded open immigration into Palestine and settlement of unoccupied territory. More significantly, for the first time the Zionists declared publicly their intention to establish a Jewish homeland or commonwealth in Palestine. Not long after the Biltmore conference, a number of United States senators and members of Congress signed a letter to President Franklin Roosevelt supporting Jewish rights in Palestine. In 1944, less than two years later, the U.S. Congress passed a joint resolution endorsing the Biltmore program. The same year, the British Labor Party recommended that their government encouraged the immigration of European Jews to Palestine. In August 1945, President Harry S. Truman requested the British Prime Minister to allow one hundred thousand European Jews to emigrate to Palestine. This quick succession of events and their profound and lasting consequences marked a death knell for the indigenous inhabitants of Palestine.

In 1946, a year after World War II ended, the United States and the British government formed a commission to investigate conditions in Palestine. The Anglo-American Commission, also known as the Morrison-Grady Commission, recommended the conversion of the Palestine Mandate into a trusteeship divided into two autonomous Jewish and Arab provinces, with Jerusalem and the Naqab Desert to remain under the control of the British government. Although the British were in favor of the proposal, the Palestinians, the Zionists, and the United States rejected the plan. The British also fought United States and Zionist pressure to allow another one hundred thousand immigrants to enter into Palestine.

In the meantime, tension between Zionists and the British Administration continued to escalate. Local Jews taunted British soldiers and likened them to Nazis. In response, the soldiers, on a number of occasions, entered Jewish settlements and scrawled swastikas and anti-Semitic slogans on the walls.

Increased terrorism by Zionist groups, the majority of it directed toward the British, played a significant role in heightening the already seething tension. In 1945, the Irgun attacked two British police stations, leaving nine officers dead. David Ben-Gurion and other mainstream Zionist leaders condemned the attack, nevertheless, additional attacks followed. In April 1946, seven British soldiers were killed. And, in July of the same year an act of terrorism of international proportion exploded across the front pages of every major newspaper in the world. The Irgun blew up a wing of the King David Hotel in Jerusalem. The bomb exploded in that portion of the hotel that the British used as military headquarters. The explosion killed ninety-one people, Jews, Arabs, and British. By the end of the year Jewish terrorist groups claimed to have killed three hundred and seventy-three people. Three hundred were civilians. In this atmosphere of increasing violence and uncertainly both the Palestinian and Jewish communities prepared for armed conflict.

The only thing that was for certain during the years immediately following the war is that British authority in the Middle East, and particularly in Palestine, was beginning to erode. After their failure to suppress the Zionist revolt it became clearer and clearer that the British were under siege and in retreat. Although they made a concerted effort to suppress the Zionist revolt, it was a feeble effort compared to the massive assaults they launched against the Palestinians back in 1936. British forces killed thousands of Palestinians during the Arab

Revolt. In contrast, between August 1945 and September 1947, thirty-seven Jewish terrorists and one hundred and sixty-nine British soldiers died. In 1936, Palestinian leaders and members of the Arab Higher Committee were arrested, detained, or deported, and the committee was outlawed for eight years. The leaders of the Zionist revolt were detained for less than three months. Whatever the reasons for these discrepancies, they showed clear signs that the British were no longer in control of the situation in Palestine.

Less than a year after the explosion at the King David Hotel, the British government decided to withdraw its troops, relinquish control of Palestine, and turn over responsibility for the mandate to the United Nations, an international organization composed of most of the countries of the world. It was founded in 1945 with the stated purpose to promote peace, security, and economic development. The United Nations is the successor to the League of Nations, the international organization formed after World War I.

On November 29, 1947, the United Nations General Assembly voted Resolution 181 on the "Future Government of Palestine," which partitioned Palestine into an Arab and Jewish state. Strangely enough, the United Nations partition plan coincided, almost to the letter, to the plan the Zionists had unveiled at the Biltmore Hotel Conference in 1942. This was the same plan that had been endorsed by the United States in August of 1946.

In 1947, the Jewish community constituted thirty-one percent of the total population of Palestine, nevertheless, the United Nations Resolution granted the proposed Jewish state fifty-five percent of historic Palestine. The proposed Palestinian state, in contrast, was awarded forty-five percent of the land of Palestine. Jerusalem and Bethlehem were supposed to be separate entities under the administration of an international authority. As expected, Palestinians and other Arabs were outraged and rejected outright the United Nations Resolution.

Palestine was engulfed in war almost as soon as the United Nations resolution was passed. November 30, 1947, the day following the Resolution, violent confrontations erupted between Arabs and Jews in Haifa, Tel Aviv, Jaffa, Lydda, and Jerusalem. There were also rebellions in Beirut, Aleppo, Damascus, Baghdad, and a number of other Arab cities outside Palestine. Al-Hajj Amin al-Husseini had reestablished the Arab Higher Committee in Cairo and then moved it to Beirut and from the Lebanese capital he declared the United Nation Resolution to be *"null and void"* and it would not under any circumstances be respected by the Palestinian people. With British forces in preparation to withdraw from Palestine, the Palestinians used the opportunity to raise a guerrilla army and resist the implementation of the partition resolution. The guerrilla army was supported by a network of local committees devoted to fund-raising, and recruitment. By March 1948, the guerrillas had been reinforced by the arrival of nearly seven thousand volunteers from neighboring Arab countries. The forces were known as the Arab Liberation Army.

But even with these reinforcements the Palestinian and Arab forces were severely out-numbered, out-armed, and out-trained. Jewish forces had tanks, armored cars, fighter planes, and field guns. They also had the upper hand in training, technical knowledge, experience, firepower, and mobility. From the start the Palestinians were unprepared politically and militarily to defend the integrity and unity of their country. Given these circumstances the outcome of this armed conflict was inevitable.

Beginning in April 1948, the Jewish military launched massive assaults against Palestinian forces. Through terror, psychological warfare, and direct conquest, the Palestinian people endured one of the worse defeats in the history of their struggle for independence. Entire villages were destroyed and massive numbers of Palestinians were sent into exile.

On May 14, 1948, the Zionists declared the State of Israel, eleven minutes later, President Harry S. Truman, recognized the sovereign State of Israel. With these events the State of Israel came into existence. For the Jewish people this was the fulfillment of a Zionist vision. For the indigenous inhabitants of Palestine this was al-Nakbah, Palestine's catastrophic destruction. More profoundly, it was the beginning of the Palestinian Diaspora that would last into the next century.

Arab Villagers Evacuate Homes, c. 1948

With the creation of Israel, most of Palestine's Arab population was forced into exile.
Between 750,000 and 800,000 became refugees, settling in areas later known as the
West Bank and the Gaza Strip. Others found refuge in neighboring Arab countries.

9

The Palestinian Diaspora

l-Nakbah meant the destruction of Palestinian society. It also meant the dispossession, dispersal, and destitution of the Palestinian people, a process that began in 1800 and ended one hundred and forty-eight years later. From a total population of 900,00 Palestinians in areas occupied by Israel, 750,000 to 800,000 became refugees. In a matter of less than a month during the spring of 1948, the lives of generations of families, of mothers and fathers, and children, had been completely dispossessed and disrupted. Their homes had been destroyed, blown to bits and incinerated by a cascading avalanche of exploding bombs. The pictures they had hanging on their walls, the books that lined their shelves, the plates they ate supper from each night were all gone.

Their mementos and precious keepsakes that were passed down from one generation to the next, were ground into dust beneath the boots of invading enemies, and the wheels of metal, unstoppable death machines spitting fires, bombs, and bullets. That is the meaning of al-Nakbah for the Palestinians, suffering that evades understanding. One people's victory is another people's death and destruction.

After al-Nakbah, the people of Palestine were divided into three distinct but widely dispersed areas. Between 100,00 and 180,000 Palestinians remained in their homes and on the land in what became Israel. Another 50,000 people remained behind Arab military lines in east central Palestine and the Gaza Strip. Finally, more than 750,000 became refugees in east central Palestine, later known as the West Bank, the Gaza Strip, and neighboring Arab countries. For example, 10,000 Palestinians were given sanctuary in Egypt and another 80,000 went to Syria.

No matter where it was that they found refuge, the circumstances of Palestinians who left their homes added new depths of suffering to an already unbearable crisis. This was primarily because most Palestinians left their homes and villages on short notice, and most assumed their leaving would be temporary, just like a hundred times before when the never-ending conflict between the two opposing communities erupted into violent confrontation. Few if any Palestinians realized or understood that this time events would turn out differently. For these reasons they took few possessions and were not prepared materially or psychologically for a long absence away from the people, places, and things that had been the central focus of their lives only the day before. To make matters worse, once they had been driven from their homes and their possessions, they were consistently prevented from returning to their communities of origin. It was not only the uncertainties caused by the danger, threats, and violence of war that kept them away, but also the deliberate and intentional policies of the new state of Israel. And the leaders of Israel defended these policies on the basis that the security of their country would be endangered by the return of hundreds of thousands of Arabs committed to the destruction of the Jewish state. In an effort to make sure these policies remained intact, Israeli forces destroyed abandoned Palestinian villages, both to prevent their return and to prepare the land for settlement by Jews. In many cases Palestinian property was wantonly destroyed, and there was large-scale looting, as well as instances of destruction of villages without apparent military necessity.

Without a doubt, the effect of the dispossession and displacement of the Palestinian population was devastating. Refugees, after a difficult and perilous journey, often found themselves in camps and centers that were ill equipped to meet their needs. The Red Cross and the Red Crescent, along with numerous other charitable organizations attempted to bring relief to an ever-increasing population of dispossessed.

The devastation caused by the Palestinian Diaspora and the effects it had upon the Palestinian people should not be underestimated. The depth of human suffering was tremendous as this poignant account of one family's misfortunes so eloquently testifies:

> We came to Lebanon and life was not what we expected it to be. Conditions were bad. We had nothing to live on. I became desperate, and one night I decided to leave my family and go back to the village to get some money I had buried outside my house before the Jews attacked. But I never reached my village. I was caught by the Jews and put in Jail.

This is just one of the literally hundreds if not thousands of testimonies of the horror and tragedy that the Palestinian people suffered in the aftermath of the 1947-1948 War. All paint a vivid and moving portrait of the experiences, which shaped and continue to shape Palestinian personal and political outlook. Indeed, the Palestinian Diaspora, the loss of the Palestinian homeland, and the dispossession and dispersal of the indigenous people of the sacred and historic earth known as Palestine, are themes that resonate throughout the art and literature and political writings of the Palestinian people like a song of sorrow. Even now, in the twenty-first century, a half-century's journey from al-Nakbab, Palestinian thoughts and feelings echo the tragic loss of their hopes, and dreams, and freedom. And they are driven by a strong and bitter passion to reclaim what they feel belongs to them by birthright. It is the expression of this terrible and painful passion that explodes into vivid, violent images and newspaper headlines. A passion that cannot be dismissed or denied by calling it by any other name, *"terrorism"* is the one most often used. And, if the past fifty years are any indication, it is also a passion that will not be conquered by bombs and bullets and killing machines.

In the years before al-Nakbah, the two dominant themes that fueled the conflict between the Palestinian people and the Jewish community, was immigration and land acquisition. During the years following the 1947-1948 War, the two most important issues that dominated Palestinian thought and action were concerns regarding the legitimacy of the State of Israel. The second was concerned with the fate of the Palestinian refugees.

From the beginning of this new phase of the conflict, Palestinians and Arabs from other countries argued that the establishment of a Jewish state in Palestine was an illegal and illegitimate act. Palestinians and Arabs who held this point of view likened the Jewish occupation of Palestine to that of a group of strangers who invades and takes possession of another person's house. They pointed out that Palestine had been an Arab country for hundreds of years, until the organized immigration of Jews from Russia, Eastern and Western Europe. They also believed that this mass immigration was orchestrated by Zionists for the sole purpose of establishing a Jewish homeland, even if that meant dislodging the indigenous inhabitants of Palestine. In their version of the story, the Jews invaded and then occupied the house of the Palestinians, against their will. This feat was accomplished with strategic intervention of European colonial powers, especially the aid and comfort of the British Empire and in response to the claim that the people of Palestine had benefited from the invasion and occupation of their "house," representatives of the Palestinian cause bluntly replied that,

> You say we are better off, you say my house has been enriched by the strangers who have entered it. But it is my house, and I did not invite the strangers in, or ask them to enrich it, and I do not care how poor or bare it is if only I am master of it.

Of course, supporters of the State of Israel offer equally compelling arguments defending the legality and legitimacy of the Jewish state. They maintain, for example, that the Jewish people's rights to Palestine are derived from a historical connection with the land that was established four thousand years ago, when God granted Abraham and his descendants all the land of Canaan for an everlasting possession. These claims and counter claims, like the ongoing conflict between the Palestinians and the Israelis, will not be resolved by whoever builds the better case, the relationship, as violent as it has been, is much too complex for so simple a solution. But the important thing is not to let these arguments, no matter how complex and compelling, obscure the fact that Jewish political rights and statehood have been achieved at the expense of the Palestinian people. And the creation of the state of Israel is the result of the triumph by force of arms of an "alien people" over the indigenous inhabitants of Palestine. Furthermore, in theory and practice, following the dictates and aspirations of its Zionist founders, Israel, by definition is a settler colony. A settler colony, or a colony of settlement results when citizens of a foreign country migrate to and eventually take complete control of a new area. These areas came to be dominated not only by foreign people but also by foreign crops and animals. The foreign colonizers ordinarily substituted their culture for the existing one. Settlers often excluded native or indigenous inhabitants from their society or killed many of them in violent confrontations or by exposure to disease. In the Americas, Native Americans were decimated to the point of extinction from disease introduced by Europeans, diseases from which they had no immunity. Also entire groups of Native Americans were systematically killed, disposed of their land and possessions, and widely dispersed. The "Trail of Tears" is but one example. Finally, colonies of settlement were located in temperate zones, with climates similar to Europe's. They are sometimes called Neo-Europes or, until recently White Man's Countries. Examples of colonies of settlement include the British colonies in America, Virginia, Massachusetts, and Canada, and Australia. After the 1947-1948 War, Palestine could be added to this list. And, like other colonized people, Native Americans, the Maya and the Incas, the people of the African Continent, the Palestinians cannot reasonably be expected to submit to their dispossession and dispersal, not to mention their possible political and cultural extinction without putting up some kind of fight.

This, then, is the basis of the Palestinian argument

against the State of Israel. Whether right or wrong, Palestinians believe and are committed to the idea that Palestine by right belongs to its indigenous Arab population, to the Palestinian people, whose presence in their native land was undisturbed for centuries prior to the emergence of modern political Zionism. So far, no argument, bombs, and bullets have been able to shake the foundations of that belief:

> Many have been the self-appointed counselors of realism, urging upon Palestinians acknowledgement of the status quo in Palestine and acceptance of their exile "in good grace." But the people which had remained for thirty years undaunted by the combined power of British Imperialism and Zionist Colonialism, knew very well how to resist those siren-calls.
>
> The Zionist settler-state, therefore has remained a usurper, lacking even the semblance of legitimacy, because the people of Palestine has remained loyal to its heritage and faithful to its rights.
>
> And the people of Palestine knows that the pathway to the future is the liberation of its homeland.

The second issue, intricately linked to the first, that is central to the conflict between the Palestinians and Israelis is the fate of the Palestinian refugees. It is the position of the Palestinians that as a result of the 1947-1948 War, the majority of the Palestinians fled their villages, and their land primarily because of the mortal fear created by the systematic terror campaigns executed by the Israeli forces. They cite Deir Yassin as an example of the terror tactics used by the Zionist forces against the Palestinians. Deir Yassin was a Palestinian village about five miles west of Jerusalem. On April 9, 1948, Israeli forces entered the village and massacred 254 defenseless civilians, including one hundred women and children. Afterward the bodies were hacked into pieces and thrown into a well. Palestinians

"Wanted" Poster

After Zionist terror attacks on several Arab villages—some of which had non-aggression pacts with their Jewish neighbors—the Palestine Police Force issued this "Wanted" poster calling for the arrest of those believed responsible.

believe that what motivated the Israelis to commit such atrocities was that they wanted to incite panic among the Palestinian population and thereby frighten them to the point of abandoning their land, homes, and possessions. Palestinians also point out that the inhabitants of Deir Yassin were not involved in the war effort. As a matter of fact, Deir Yassin was one of several Palestinian villages that had signed a non-aggression pact with its Jewish neighbors. Finally, Palestinians also claim that after the massacre, the Irgun command sent out a congratulatory message stating *"As in Deir Yassin, so everywhere, Oh Lord, Oh Lord, you have chosen us for the conquest."*

Again, claims and counterclaims should not be allowed to obliterate one essential and simple truth, and that is, regardless of the causes of the Palestinian Diaspora, the fact remains that the Palestinian people have suffered unspeakable horror and devastation since the catastrophic destruction of the sacred homeland, Palestine. Yet, even in the depths of this destruction they have not relinquished their hope and dreams of *"the return."* In many Palestinian homes in the Diaspora, families display olive wood carvings or framed needlework pictures with the words, *"Innana raji'oun"* or *"Innana 'ai doun,"* which means *"we shall return."*

Arab and Jewish Mothers of Children Killed in the Violence, c. 1999

As reflected in the faces of these two grieving mothers—one Jewish and one Arab—the violence in Palestine has created an unenviable bond of tragedy among the peoples of the region.

10
Palestinian Authority

he years between al-Nakbah and the Six-Day War in June 1967, was a period of intense political activity in the Arab world. Political parties and movements spanned the political spectrum from one extreme to the other, from the Communist parties on the left to the conservative movements like al-Ikhwan al-Muslimin, or the Muslim Brotherhood, on the right. But the clarion call that most Arabs throughout the Middle East heard the loudest and the clearest, following the catastrophic destruction of Palestine, was secular pan-Arab nationalism, a movement both simple and difficult to define. On the most basic level it meant *"brotherhood,"* a belief that Arab people share a common bond and a common origin and should strive together to achieve their common objectives. But, at the same time it demanded something more, something deeper, a belief or philosophy that extended the boundaries of brotherhood to include other people from other countries who had shared a common or similar historical experience. Ultimately, secular pan-Arab nationalism sought to unite the developing countries of the world in a struggle for self-determination. During the decades in question, the Cold War decades, this movement helped give birth to an even larger movement referred to as the Nonaligned Movement, or NAM, which was a loose association of countries in Africa, Asia, and Latin America. One of the significant aspects of these countries who all shared a similar colonial background, was their refusal to align themselves with either one of the world powers at that time, the United States representing the capitalist or Western bloc, and the Soviet Union representing the communist or Eastern bloc.

This idea of self-sufficiency and self-determination made a big impact in the Middle East. It gave new meaning to the idea of Arab unity. It meant that the newly independent Arab states had enough in common, in shared culture and historical experience as well as shared interests to make it possible for them to come into close union and cooperation with each other. And such a union would not only give them greater collective power but would bring about that moral unity between people and government, which would make government legitimate and stable.

Palestinians also surrendered to the clarion call of pan-Arab nationalism and became actively involved in the struggle to regain their homeland in spite of the lack of independent Palestinian organizations. In fact, the Arab Nationalist Movement (ANM) was founded and organized by Palestinian students at the American University of Beirut in Lebanon. ANM was headed by George Habash who later founded another organization called Popular Front for the Liberation of Palestine, or PFLP.

It was in 1956, during the Suez War that the Palestinian Liberation movement received its greatest boost. By the mid-1950s the Egyptian government had become a major supporter of the Palestinian struggle to regain their homeland. Egypt also refused to allow Israeli ships to use the Suez Canal and in 1951 blockaded the Strait of Tiran, Israel's access to the Red Sea, which Israel regarded as an act of war. In June 1956 Egypt nationalized the Suez Canal, which had been jointly owned by Britain and France. In late October, Israel invaded the Gaza Strip and the Sinai Peninsula. Britain and France attacked Egypt a few days later. Although the fighting was brief and Israel was forced to withdraw from both the Gaza Strip and the Sinai, the conflict further inflamed regional tensions.

For Palestinians, the collective experience of defending themselves against Israel only eight years after al-Nakbah was all the catalyst needed to inspire the emergence of an independent Palestinian militant movement. In fact, a popular resistance movement erupted in the Gaza Strip in reaction to Israel's invasion and occupation of the territory during the Suez War. The movement was aided by the military training and technical assistance Palestinians received from the Egyptian army. As a result, Palestinian rebels launched several successful guerrilla raids across the borders into Israel, similar to the raids Israeli terrorist launched against the British prior to their withdrawal from Palestine.

Following the success of these initial raids, Palestinians in the Gaza Strip and elsewhere began independent, clandestine campaigns of political organizing and military training. "In the absence of a government to defend them, Palestinians throughout the Diaspora began to reassemble the pieces of their shattered political, economic, and social structures. The institutions they revived or reconstructed, women's teacher's students' and workers' organizations as well as charitable societies, were the natural heirs of the pre-1948 institutions."

The most important of the guerrilla groups during this period was Fatah, the Palestinian National Liberation Movement, whose name is an acronym from Harakat al-Tahrir al-Filastini (Palestinian Liberation Movement), the order of the initials being reversed. Active during the mid-1950s, Fatah was initially a loose network of Palestinian groups in refugee camps, Palestinian communities, and student groups. Yasir Arafat, Salah Khalaf, and Khalil al-Wazir or Abu Jihad, were among its founding members. The movement began to take shape at meetings held in Kuwait in October 1957 but did not come into its full power until several years later, especially after the Six-Day War in 1967. The movement's publication, *Filastinuna,* or *Our Palestine,* first appeared in 1959. Because of its subversive nature Fatah was forced to operate underground even in Arab states that supported Palestinian liberation.

Almost simultaneously, while Fatah and other guerrilla groups carried out a clandestine warfare, al-Hajj Amin al-Husseini, the former mufti of Palestine and president of the Arab Higher Committee, appealed to the League of Arab States to help establish an independent Palestinian state. The League of Arab States, also informally known as the Arab League, is a voluntary association of independent Arab countries. Its stated purposes are to strengthen ties between member states, coordinate their policies, and promote their common interest. The League was founded in 1945 by Egypt, Iraq, Lebanon, Saudi Arabia, Syria, Transjordan, and Yemen. Jordan joined in 1949, as did many other Arab and African countries over the years. As a point of fact the Palestine Liberation Organization became an official member in 1976. The League is a prime example of secular pan-Arab nationalism in action.

In the meantime, members of the League of Arab States voted unanimously to create a *"kiyan,"* a political organization that would speak and act on behalf of the Palestinian people.

To initiate this process the Palestinian Liberation Army came into existence, units of which would be under the jurisdiction and commands of various Arab militaries. Perhaps even more important, in January 1964, during the first Arab summit ever, called to discuss Israel's plan to divert the waters of the Jordan River, the Palestinian representative of the Arab League, Amad al-Shuqayri was authorized to convene a new Palestine National Council, or legislative congress. The appointed council met in Jerusalem and founded the Palestine Liberation Organization, or PLO, as its executive branch. The stated purpose for the founding of the PLO was to formulate plans for the establishment of a Palestinian entity that would contribute more broadly to the struggle against the Jewish State.

The PLO was founded to establish a more legitimate and organized channel for Palestinian nationalism that then was offered by independent guerrilla groups. Later some of these groups joined the PLO, including Fatah. Professional, labor, and student groups also joined the PLO, but over time, during the course of its evolution, it has been the *fedayeen*, or guerrilla faction, that has exerted the greatest influence within the Palestine Liberation Organization.

The PLO is made up of three main bodies: (1) the fifteen-member Executive Committee, which makes decisions and which includes representatives of the PLO's majar fedayeen, or guerrilla forces, (2) the sixty-member central committee, which is an advisory body and (3) the 599-member Palestine National Council, which has historically been seen as an assembly of the Palestinian people. Before the creation of the Palestinian National Authority, or PNA, which was founded in 1993, the PLO also had departments and agencies that provided military, health, information, finance, education, and other services to the dispersed Palestinian population. Since 1994, however, the PNA has taken over these functions.

The PLO grew in prominence after Israel gained control of the largely Palestinian-inhabited West Bank and Gaza Strip in June 1967. The Arab-Israeli war, remembered for all time as the Six-Day War, changed the course of history not only for the Palestinian people struggling to regain their homeland, but for all the independent Arab states throughout the Middle East. It also delivered a devastating blow to the idea and philosophy of secular pan-Arab nationalism. In six short days, the nationalist Arab republics of Egypt, Syria, Iraq, and Jordan were defeated by the State of Israel. These Arab republics had been united in their commitment to the Arab peoples to fight for political independence, economic well-being through jobs and education, and a general sense of self-determination for every man, women, and child, especially the people of the Palestinian Diaspora. After the Six-Day War with Israel all of these hopes and dreams were shattered. For the Palestinians it was their second devastating defeat in twenty years.

Besides the unrelenting sense of shame and humiliation of being handed such a profound and devastating defeat at the hands of their sworn enemy, there were several other lasting consequences of the Six-Day War. First and foremost, it left the Arab world reeling from such an unexpected and decisive defeat. A general sense of doom and hopelessness pervaded everything Arab, thick and heavy like a layer of dust after a sandstorm in the desert. It was more terrible than the grief of death, this defeat with the victory drums of their enemy pounding hard and heavy with the rhythm of joy and celebration. One people's defeat and devastation is another people's victory.

The war changed the balance of power not only between Israel and the surrounding Arab states but also between the secular pan-Arab nationalists, and the more conservative oil-exporting monarchies of the Arabian

Peninsula. This created a regional political vacuum and gave the fedayeen the opportunity to forge ahead with their own special method of waging political and military warfare. In other words, they became, perhaps for the first time in recent history, independent agents in the Palestinian, Arab, and Middle Eastern arenas. This would prove to be another crucial turning point in the Palestinian liberation struggle. Because the fedayeen seemed the only ones willing and capable to forge ahead during this time of moral, spiritual, and political crisis their revolutionary ideology became the new clarion call and spread widely and deeply within the communities of the Palestinian Diaspora and throughout the Arab world.

But they were not to rule the day alone. The conservative Arab monarchies that felt almost as threatened by the new Arab revolution as they did by Israel, also emerged from beneath the shadow of the defeated secular pan-Arab nationalism. As a result, two opposing factions emerged in the Middle East. One was revolutionary and led by the Palestinians, the other conservative and accommodationist, led by Saudi Arabia and a defeated and chastened Arab nationalist Egypt of Abdel-Nasser who, before the 1967 defeat, had represented the vanguard of the liberation struggle. This conflict between two opposing ideas would define the boundaries of the Palestinian Liberation struggle for the next four decades.

In March 1968, less than a year after the Six-Day War, the PLO fedayeen won fame by repelling an Israeli attack on PLO bases in Jordan. A year later, Yasir Arafat, the leader of Fatah, was elected chairman of the PLO.

After being named chairman of the PLO in 1969, Arafat became commander in chief of the Palestinian Revolutionary Forces in 1971 and, two years later, head of the PLO's political department. From that point forward, he directed his efforts increasingly toward political persuasion rather than

Yasir Arafat, c. 1998

Since 1968, the face of Yasir Arafat has appeared on newspapers, magazines, and television screens around the world. As the leader of the Palestine Liberation Organization (PLO), Arafat has set policy for Arab Palestinians, though his control over his people's actions may often seem tenuous.

confrontation and terrorism against Israel. In November 1974, Arafat became the first representative of a nongovernmental organization to address a session of the United Nations General Assembly. During the same year the Arab Nations at an Arab League Summit in Rabat, Morocco, recognized the PLO as the sole legitimate representative of the Palestinian people. Both of these events were significant victories but diplomatic victories alone did little to change the nature of the conflict between the Palestinians and the State of Israel. In 1982, Israel invaded Lebanon. This invasion was directed against the PLO, intensified internal conflicts, and forced twelve thousand PLO members to flee once more, this time to several Arab countries.

Discontented and disillusioned by the PLO's efforts to achieve any significant gains, in 1987 Palestinians in the Gaza Strip began a spontaneous revolt against Israel, known as the *intifada*. *Intifada*, Arabic for *"throwing off,"* was an attempt by Palestinians to liberate portions of Palestine through a combination of force and negotiations. However, as the intifada continued it grew in strength and the forceful or violent aspects of the uprising was stressed. As the intifada grew more violent the Israeli military responded in kind. In time, the violence and destruction, and international pressure forced both sides to attempt a more diplomatic solution.

The intifada was a factor leading to the September 1993 Oslo Accords between the PLO and Israel. This agreement led to Palestinian self-rule in the Gaza Strip and the West Bank town of Jericho under the direction of the newly created Palestinian National Authority, headed by Yasir Arafat. A second agreement signed in September 1995, extended Palestinian self-rule to most of the remaining Palestinian towns and refugee camps in the West Bank.

Arafat continued as chairman of the Palestine National Authority until its first election was held in January 1996. Following these elections, an overwhelming majority elected Yasir Arafat president. It was at this moment that the Palestinian Authority, an independent state, governed by the will of the Palestinian people, was born. Although several years of relative calm ensued, this by no means marked the end of the story or the end of the conflict.

3000–2000 B.C. Arrival and settlement of the Canaanites

1250 B.C. Israelite conquest of Canaan.

1000–961 B.C. King David

965–928 B.C. King Solomon (Sulayman) construction of the Temple of Jerusalem.

928 B.C. Division of the Israelites into the Kingdom of Israel and Judah.

721 B.C. Assyrian conquest of Israel

586 B.C. Judah defeated by Babylonians under King Nebuchadnezzar. Deportation of Jews into Babylon, and destruction of the Temple.

539 B.C. Persia conquers Babylon, allows Jews to return to Israel. Construction of new Temple.

333 B.C. Alexander the Great conquers Persia. Palestine comes under Greek rule.

323 B.C. Alexander the Great dies. Ptolemies of Egypt followed by Seleucids of Syria rule Palestine.

165 B.C. Maccabees revolt against the Seleucid ruler and establish independent state.

63 B.C. Palestine becomes part of the Roman Empire.

70 A.D. Destruction of Second Temple by Roman Emperor Titus.

132–135 A.D. Suppression of Bar Kohhba Revolt. Jews barred from Jerusalem and Emperor Hadrian builds a pagan city on its ruins.

330–638 A.D. Palestine ruled by Byzantine Empire. The spread of Christianity.

638 A.D. Omar ibn al-Khattaab enters Jerusalem and ends Byzantine rule.

661–750 A.D. Palestine becomes a province under the Arab-Islamic Umayyad Dynasty that was based in Damascus.

6685–691 A.D. The Umayyad Caliph Abdul Malik Ibn Marwan (685–705) builds the Dome of the Rock in Jerusalem.

705 A.D. al-Walid Ibn Abdul Malik (705-715) of the Umayyads builds al-Aqsa Mosque in Jerusalem.

750–1258   Palestine becomes a province Abbasid Dynasty.

1099–1187   The Crusaders invade Palestine and establish the Latin Kingdom of Jerusalem.

1187   The Battle of Hittin in Palestine. Saladin of Egypt defeats the Crusaders and liberates Palestine from European Control.

1517   Ottoman conquest of most of the Arab world including Palestine.

1517–1918   Palestine under Ottoman rule.

1882–1904   First wave of immigration of Jewish settlers to Palestine.

1897   First Zionist congress meets in Basel, Switzerland.

1904–1914   Second wave of immigration of Jewish settlers to Palestine.

1911   *Filistine* newspaper founded in Jaffa by Issa al-Issa.

1914   World War I starts.

1915–1916   Sharif Hussein and Henry McMahon exchange correspondence guaranteeing Arab independence.

1916   Britain and France sign Sykes-Picot Agreement, which divides the Ottoman Middle East provinces among them, on May 16.

1917   Lord Arthur Balfour, British foreign secretary, sends a letter (later known as the Balfour Declaration) to Lord Edmund de Rothschild supporting the establishment of a Jewish national home in Palestine.

1918   British forces led by General Allenby occupy Palestine. World War I ends in October.

1919   First National Conference-Palestine. King-Crane Commission.

1920   San Remo Conference grants Great Britain Mandate over Palestine on April 24.

1922   Council of the League of Nations Mandate for Palestine on July 24.

1936–1939   Arab Revolt erupts in Palestine.

1937   The Peel Commission Report recommends the partition of Palestine.

1939   The British government issues MacDonald White Paper restricting Jewish immigration.

1942   Biltmore Hotel Conference on May 11.

1946–1948   Jewish-Palestinian-British War breaks out.

1948   The al-Nakbah or catastrophic destruction of Palestine and the beginning of Palestinian Diaspora. Zionists declare the Independent State of Israel.

1949   At the end of the 1947-1948 War, Israel extends its holdings of Palestine.

1950   The West Bank becomes part of Jordan.

1953   Israel launches a large-scale assault on the Gaza Strip.

1956   Suez War.

1957   Yasir Arafat helps found the Palestine Liberation Movement, whose name becomes Fatah.

1964   The Palestine Liberation Organization is founded.

1967   The Six-Day War.

1968   The Battle of al-karameh in which Palestinian guerrillas prevent Israel from occupying the Gaza Strip.

1974   PLO Chairman Yasir Arafat addresses the United Nations General Assembly.

1978   The Israeli army invades Lebanon, demolishes villages, and kills hundreds of Lebanese and Palestinians.

1982   The Israelis army invades Lebanon to destroy the military, political, and institutional infrastructure of the PLO.

1987   The Palestinian intifada begins in Gaza and spreads to the West Bank.

1991   The United States and its allies attack Iraq, forcing Iraq to withdraw from Kuwait in the Gulf War.

1993   The PLO establishes the Palestinian Authority and appoints Arafat as its head.

1994   The Palestinian Authority holds its first meeting in Gaza city Arafat, Rabin, and Peres accept the Nobel Peace Prize.

1996   Palestinian Elections. Palestinian legislative council founded. Yasir Arafat elected president of the Palestinian Authority.

1997   Palestinian Authority and Israel sign the Protocol concerning the redeployment in Hebron (Hebron Agreement).

1998 Palestinian Authority and Israel sign the Wye River Memorandum.

1999 King Hussein of Jordan dies. Palestine and Israel sign the Sharm el-Sheikh Memorandum (Known as Wye II).

2000 Palestinian-Israeli negotiations at Camp David begin July 11. Ariel Sharon visits the Haram el-Sharif in Jerusalem igniting a series of violent clashes known as al-Aqsa Intifada.

2001 Sharon is elected prime minister of Israel.

2002 More failed talks. Palestine and Israel engaged in violent confrontation for past eighteen months, since the election of Sharon.

Bernards, Neal and JoAnne Buggey (conslt.) *The Palestinian Conflict: Identifying Propaganda Techniques.* San Diego. Greenhaven Press, 1990.

Dimbleby, Jonathan. *The Palestinians.* New York: Quartet Books, Inc., 1979.

Gendzier, Irene L. *A Middle East Reader.* New York: Pegasus, 1969.

Hadawi, Sami. *Bitter Harvest: A Modern History of Palestine.* New York: Olive Branch Press, 1991.

LaQueur, Walter and Barry Rubin (ed.) *The Israeli-Arab Reader: A Documentary History of The Middle East Conflict.* New York: Penguin Boods, 1976.

Said, Edward W. *The Question of Palestine.* New York: Vintage Books, 1992.

Segeu, Tom. *One Palestine Complete: Jews and Arabs Under the British Mandate.* New York: Henry Holt E. Company, 1999.

Britannica 2002 Encyclopedia.

Encarta 2002 Encyclopedia.

Farsoun, Samik K. and Christinia E. Zacharia. *Palestine and the Palestinians.* Boulder. Westview Press, 1997.

Dimbleby, Jonathan. *The Palestinians.* New York. Quartet Books, Inc., 1979.

Gerner, Deborah J. *One Land, Two Peoples: The Conflict Over Palestine.* Boulder. Westview Press, 1991.

Hadawi. Sami. *Bitter Harvest: A Modern History of Palestine.* New York. Olive Branch Press, 1991.

Said, Edward W. *The Question of Palestine.* New York. Vintage Books 1992.

Smith, Charles D. *Palestine and The Arab-Israeli Conflict.* New York. St. Martin's Press, 1992.

Tessler, Mark. *A History of The Israeli-Palestinian Conflict.* Bloomington. Indiana University Press, 1994.

JOHN G. HALL received a Bachelor's degree in African American Studies and American Literature from the University of Massachusetts in Boston, and a Master's Degree in Education from Converse College in Spartanburg, South Carolina. He has contributed fiction, nonfiction and poetry to *African Voices, Aim Magazine, BackHome, Black Diaspora, Listen Magazine*, and *The Sounds of Poetry*. John and his wife Brenda live with their daughter, Jessie McDonnell-Hall, in the mountains of Western North Carolina.

AKBAR S. AHMED holds the Ibn Khaldun Chair of Islamic Studies at the School of International Service of American University. He is actively involved in the study of global Islam and its impact on contemporary society. He is the author of many books on contemporary Islam, including *Discovering Islam: Making Sense of Muslim History and Society,* which was the basis for a six-part television program produced by the BBC called *Living Islam*. Ahmed has been visiting professor and the Stewart Fellow in the Humanities at Princeton University, as well as visiting professor at Harvard University and Cambridge University.